STUDY GUIDE

Economic
Analysis

& CANADIAN POLICY

Seventh Edition

STUDY GUIDE

Economic Analysis

& CANADIAN POLICY

Seventh Edition

David Stager
University of Toronto

Butterworths
Toronto and Vancouver

Study Guide
Economic Analysis and Canadian Policy
© Butterworths Canada 1992

Printed and bound in Canada by
John Deyell Company Limited

Canadian Cataloguing in Publication Data

Stager, David, 1937-
Economic analysis & Canadian policy, seventh
edition. Study guide

Supplement to: Stager, David, 1937- .
Economic analysis & Canadian policy. 7th ed.
ISBN 0-409-89946-1

1. Economics - Problems, exercises, etc.
2. Canada - Economic policy - Problems,
exercises, etc. I. Title.

HB171.5.S72 1991   330   C91-095416-X

Sponsoring Editor: Craig Laudrum
Development Editor: Edward O'Connor
Editor: Julia Keeler
Cover Design: Brant Cowie
Production: Kevin Skinner
Cover Photograph: Patterson/Masterfile

The Butterworth Group of Companies

Canada
Butterworths Canada Ltd., 75 Clegg Road, MARKHAM, Ont. L6G 1A1 and
409 Granville Street, Suite 1455, VANCOUVER, B.C. V6C 1T2

Australia
Butterworths Pty Ltd., SYDNEY, MELBOURNE, BRISBANE, ADELAIDE,
PERTH, CANBERRA and HOBART

Ireland
Butterworth (Ireland) Ltd., DUBLIN

New Zealand
Butterworths of New Zealand Ltd., WELLINGTON and AUCKLAND

Puerto Rico
Equity de Puerto Rico, Inc., HATO REY

Singapore
Malayan Law Journal Pte. Ltd., SINGAPORE

United Kingdom
Butterworth & Co. (Publishers) Ltd., LONDON and EDINBURGH

United States
Butterworth Legal Publishers, AUSTIN, Texas; BOSTON, Massachusetts;
CLEARWATER, Florida (D & S Publishers); ORFORD, New Hampshire
(Equity Publishing); ST. PAUL, Minnesota; and SEATTLE, Washington.

Before You Begin

A FEW WORDS OF EXPLANATION AND SUGGESTION may help you make better use of this book. The purpose of this study guide is to develop a better understanding of the concepts, theories, and policies presented in an introductory economics course—and especially in a course using *Economic Analysis and Canadian Policy,* seventh edition.

There are many approaches to the study of economics, but the basic stages in anyone's approach are likely to be fairly similar. You should rely on a combination of the textbook, your lecture notes, and these exercises. No one source is sufficient. This is particularly true of any workbook or study guide because not all of the important concepts can be included appropriately in the format of multiple-choice and true/false questions or problems. When you begin a new chapter or a new section of the course, browse through that chapter of the text, taking note of the headings, sections printed in colour, and diagrams and their captions. Read the chapter summary, but do not worry if some parts make little sense at that stage. In this initial survey you will begin to see the main themes and the important concepts that are discussed in the section. Next, read and re-read a few pages—or only parts of a page—just before your class if you are in a lecture course. Try to identify specific sections or ideas that you do not understand; read the preceding and following paragraphs carefully to see whether the problem can be resolved in this larger context.

Read the chapter completely again, breaking it into the major sections, so that you can grasp the "big picture" within which the specific details have been explained. Briefly, you should go from the general to the specific and back to the general again. Only when you feel fairly confident that you understand each chapter or section should you then proceed to the review exercises.

The chapters in this study guide correspond to the chapters in the textbook. Each chapter begins with a list of the important terms and concepts that you should be able to define or explain before proceeding further. The multiple-choice questions are to be answered with the "most appropriate" statement among those offered. For some questions, no statement may be 100 per cent satisfactory as an answer, but one statement should stand out as a better answer than any other.

The problems vary in format and purpose. Some problems are short and simply review specific ideas; others are longer and include several parts to guide you through the same logical development of a conclusion that is presented in the textbook. In other cases it is also possible to extend some topics beyond the treatment they receive in the text. Some problems require you to make calculations, plot the data, and draw conclusions. This is not simply to test your arithmetic skills. Try to see how the successive steps in each problem are related to the text's discussion of various factors and their interrelationships. Look for the general concepts and conclusions that are illustrated by the specific numerical examples.

Answers to the multiple-choice and true/false questions and problems are included in this book, but you will find it most beneficial not to look at the answers until you have completed the assignment. Then look carefully at questions where you had incorrect answers to see whether you should review those topics before proceeding.

Discussion questions at the end of each chapter have several purposes. Some questions serve as a final review, or present a different perspective on an idea. Other questions are intended as "thought-provokers": they ask you to think about your own experience within the economics framework you have just learned, or they challenge you to think beyond the concise discussion in the text. When you are asked to explain your answer, provide the detailed reasoning that leads to your conclusion.

Be sure to ask questions about anything that puzzles you. There may still be ambiguities lurking in the questions or answers, or you may have a plausible interpretation that was not anticipated. If you or your instructor do discover such difficulties or incorrect answers, please bring these to my attention by writing to me in care of the publisher. I am greatly indebted to the students in my own classes who have helped to improve these exercises; to the several instructors who tested most of these questions in their classes and made important suggestions and corrections; and to other instructors who have written with useful comments for additional exercises.

Contents

PART ONE

Economics and The Market Place

1 Economics: The Analysis of Choice

IMPORTANT TERMS AND CONCEPTS

Be sure you can define or explain each of these terms before proceeding with the questions and problems.

economics
economic resources
factors of production
commodity
intermediate vs. final goods
producer vs. consumer goods
economic vs. free goods
services
consumption
utility
production
scarcity
opportunity cost
production-possibilities boundary
consumption-possibilities curve

economic decisions or problems
technology
economic growth
economic systems
traditional economy
planned economy
market economy
price system
market
mixed economies

Appendix:

coordinate graph
dependent variable
independent variable

MULTIPLE-CHOICE QUESTIONS

Circle the letter corresponding with the most appropriate answer for each question.

1. Economics is the study of how to use:

   (a) limited resources to satisfy limited wants
   (b) unlimited resources to satisfy limited wants
   (c) limited resources to satisfy virtually unlimited wants
   (d) virtually unlimited resources to satisfy virtually unlimited wants

2. The quantity of one good that must be given up when more of another good is produced is described as:

   (a) substitute goods
   (b) opportunity cost
   (c) economy of scale
   (d) efficient production

3. A production-possibilities boundary illustrates the principle that:

   (a) an economy will automatically move to the full utilization of all its productive resources
   (b) if an economy is making the maximum use of all available resources, more of one good can be produced only if less of another good is produced
   (c) an economy can produce more as its population increases
   (d) different economies have different production possibilities

4. If the production-possibilities boundary were a straight line joining the vertical and horizontal axes, this would mean that:

   (a) the two goods concerned are produced in equal amounts
   (b) the two goods are sold at the same market prices
   (c) there must be some unemployment of labour
   (d) the opportunity cost of each good is constant regardless of the level of output of each good

5. An outward shift of the production-possibilities boundary would likely occur if:

   (a) unemployment was reduced
   (b) there was an increase in the level of technical training of the labour force
   (c) consumer wants were increased
   (d) the composition of the population shifted such that there were more full-time students and fewer workers

6. If it is possible to increase the quantity produced of one good without decreasing the quantity produced of any other good:

   (a) the economy is producing at its maximum efficiency
   (b) the economy is beyond its production-possibilities boundary
   (c) the opportunity cost of the good is zero
   (d) it is not possible to define the production-possibilities boundary

7. The productive resources available to an economy could be increased by:

    (a) an increase in the population
    (b) an increase in net immigration
    (c) higher levels of education and training in the labour force
    (d) all of the above

8. When economists say "there are no free lunches", they mean that:

    (a) the government should not subsidize food programs for the poor
    (b) the employee pays indirectly for fringe benefits through lower wages than would be received otherwise
    (c) any good or service that is provided at no direct expense to the user nevertheless requires economic resources that could have been used for the production of other goods
    (d) they do not have an adequate theory of government services

9. In a pure market economy, economic decisions are determined by:

    (a) prices set by supply and demand conditions
    (b) prices set by governments
    (c) planners who have been given this authority
    (d) persons who control the money market and the stock market

10. An economy based on the market system requires:

    (a) self-sufficient family units
    (b) money for the exchange of goods
    (c) direction from central economic authorities
    (d) an organized interaction of buyers and sellers

TRUE/FALSE QUESTIONS

State whether each of the following statements is true or false, or whether you are uncertain because the statement may be either true or false depending on the relevant circumstances and/or assumptions. Explain the reasons for your answer in each case.

1. Intermediate goods and producer goods are the same, since both are used to make consumer goods.

2. By the "fact of scarcity", economists mean that there will always be widespread poverty in the world.

3. Opportunity cost is defined as the total dollar amount that must be spent to purchase a specific commodity.

4. In an economy that produces only wheat and cheese, introduction of a higher yielding wheat variety will reduce the relative costs of both wheat and cheese.

5. A technological improvement in the production of one good may result in the increased production of another good.

6. An economy's production-possibilities boundary may shift inward as well as outward.

7. An economy may be at a point on its production-possibilities boundary even though it has some unemployed labour.

8. An economy cannot increase its current consumption of goods and services unless it gives up some future goods and services.

9. All economies face the same basic economic problems.

10. A market economy is more productive than a planned economy.

PROBLEMS

1. Suppose that an economy faces the following production-possibilities schedule:

Alternative Combinations	A	B	C	D	E
Producer goods	60	52	32	16	0
Consumer goods	0	20	40	48	50

(a) Plot these combinations, label the points, and draw the production-possibilities boundary represented by this schedule.

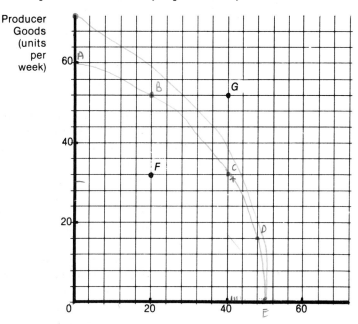

Consumer Goods (units per week)

(b) If the economy is producing the combination of goods represented by *C*, the opportunity cost of the 41st unit of consumer goods will be _____ units of producer goods. The opportunity cost of consumer goods (increases/decreases/remains constant) as the output of consumer goods increases.

(c) If the production-possibilities curve were a straight line joining points *A* and *E*, the opportunity cost of consumer goods would (increase/decrease/remain constant) with increased output of consumer goods.

(d) Combination *C* represents a (faster/slower) rate of economic growth than combination *D*.

(e) Combination _____ represents some unemployment, under-utilization of productive capacity, or otherwise inefficient production.

(f) If the economy were producing combination *F*, it would have the immediate potential for increasing its output of producer goods by _____ units without reducing the output of consumer goods.

(g) It is (possible/uncertain/impossible) that the economy could immediately produce combination G, given the existing resources and technological knowledge.

(h) Indicate with a check-mark in the appropriate column the effect each of the following events would likely have on the production-possibilities curve:

	Shift Inward	No Change	Shift Outward
(i) emigration of skilled workers	_____	_____	_____
(ii) discovery of new energy sources	_____	_____	_____
(iii) increase in size of the labour force	_____	_____	_____
(iv) increase in output of consumer goods	_____	_____	_____
(v) depletion of natural fertility of agricultural lands	_____	_____	_____

(i) Draw the new production-possibilities boundary that would result if a technological change in the production of producer goods made it possible to produce a maximum of 72 units, but there was no increase in the maximum number of consumer goods. If the economy now produces 32 units of producer goods, can it produce more consumer goods than before? Explain why or why not.

_____

_____

_____

_____

2. Suppose that the original production-possibilities boundary for an economy is represented in the diagram below as curve $x_2 y_2$.

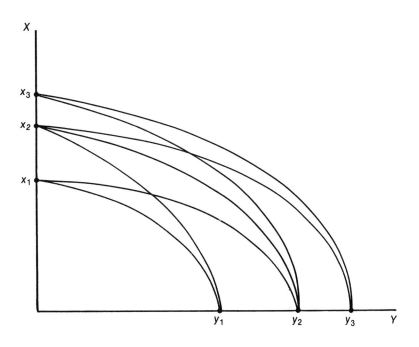

Then identify the curve that would result from each of the following:

(a) Immigration increases the skilled labour force. _____

(b) A technological improvement occurs in the production of X. _____

(c) There is a recession in the economy. _____

(d) The economy engages in international trade by exporting X and importing Y. _____

(e) Mandatory retirement is forbidden by a new charter of rights. _____

QUESTIONS FOR REVIEW AND DISCUSSION

1. Do you think it is valid to assume that not all wants can ever be satisfied? Why?

2. Canada is sometimes described as an affluent society, yet economists continue to base their analyses on the fact of scarcity. Can these two situations—affluence and scarcity—be reconciled? Explain carefully what scarcity means in this context.

3. Why is water sometimes an economic good and sometimes a free good?

4. If there were no parking meters and parking was permitted on any street, could on-street parking be considered a free good in Canadian cities? Why, or why not?

5. Why is the opportunity cost concept so important in economic analysis and economic decisions?

6. Calculate your opportunity cost for attending school or college this year.

7. What is meant by an "economic system"? What is the difference between an economic system and a political system?

8. Assume you are the chief planner in a planned economy. How will you decide what to produce, how much to produce of each commodity, and how much will be distributed to various members of the population?

9. The chapter gives a short definition for "market", but what is the meaning of the full term "market *system*"?

10. Could there ever be a pure market economy? Explain.

11. A distinction is made between "wants" and "needs" in describing the problem of scarcity. Can you think of some goods or services for which this sharp distinction cannot be made? Why is there some doubt about the category in which such goods or services should be placed?

2 Economic Analysis and Economic Policy

IMPORTANT TERMS AND CONCEPTS

Be sure you can define or explain each of these terms before proceeding with the questions and problems.

economic analysis
economic policy
positive vs. normative economics
value judgments
scientific method
laws of behaviour
theory

economic model
rational behaviour
"other things being equal"
stock vs. flow
microeconomics
macroeconomics

MULTIPLE-CHOICE QUESTIONS

Circle the letter corresponding with the most appropriate answer for each question.

1. Economic theories:

   (a) are abstract statements that are not applicable in "real world" situations
   (b) are true only for individual cases, and not for the economy as a whole
   (c) are general statements based on careful observation of facts
   (d) are useless because they are not based on laboratory experiments

2. An acceptable theory of consumer behaviour would explain:

   (a) each individual's actual behaviour
   (b) each individual's behaviour in most situations
   (c) most individuals' behaviour in most situations
   (d) all individuals' actual behaviour

3. Microeconomics is concerned with:

   (a) the aggregate level of income, employment, and output
   (b) detailed examination of separate segments of the economic system
   (c) an overall view of the operation of the economic system
   (d) the role of money in the economy

4. Economic analysis:

   (a) is another term for economic policy
   (b) refers to the normative study of economics
   (c) refers to the positive study of economics
   (d) is neither normative nor positive

5. Value judgments are essential for:

   (a) developing economic theory
   (b) determining the goals of economic policy
   (c) settling disagreements in economic theory
   (d) deciding which economic theory is more realistic

6. The concept of rational behaviour assumes that:

   (a) all individuals always try to improve their material well-being
   (b) some individuals always try to improve their material well-being
   (c) most individuals usually try to improve their material well-being
   (d) some individuals sometimes try to improve their material well-being

7. When a period of time is involved in the definition of a concept, this is an example of:

   (a) an economic law
   (b) a stock
   (c) a flow
   (d) none of the above

TRUE/FALSE QUESTIONS

State whether each of the following statements is true or false, or whether you are uncertain because the statement may be either true or false depending on the relevant circumstances and/or assumptions. Explain the reasons for your answer in each case.

1. An economic theory may be valid even though one finds occasional exceptions to it in the real world.

2. Economics cannot be very useful for analyzing individual behaviour because individuals are so different from each other.

3. Economists frequently disagree with each other because economic theory is in such a primitive state.

4. The components of an economic theory include a definition of terms, a set of assumptions, and the hypothesis about a relationship between the variables.

5. If some economic problems have not been studied extensively, one can conclude that economists have decided these problems are unimportant.

6. Economists have no laboratories; therefore, there can be no science of economics.

7. Since there is almost nothing in an economy that remains constant, the *ceteris paribus* assumption is meaningless.

PROBLEM

1. Listed below are some measures that represent either stocks or flows. Using F, S, or N, indicate which are flows, stocks, or neither:
   (a) Per capita consumption of wine in Canada per year ____
   (b) Amount of cash you now have in your purse, pocket, or wallet ____
   (c) Total value of books that you own ____
   (d) Quantity of fish caught annually by the Canadian fishing industry ____
   (e) Total annual payroll for employees of General Motors ____
   (f) Loblaws' grocery inventory for Metro Toronto ____

QUESTIONS FOR REVIEW AND DISCUSSION

1. Many House of Commons debates focus on economic issues. Should there therefore be a large proportion of economists among the MPs elected to Parliament? Why?

2. Why is it so much more difficult to decide whether governments are acting rationally than to decide whether the behaviour of consumers and producers is rational?

3. Think of three statements you have recently heard about the Canadian economy. Decide whether they are positive or normative statements, and indicate how you decided which category was most appropriate.

4. It is still necessary for economists to make explicit the assumption of rational behaviour?

3 Demand, Supply, and Market Prices

IMPORTANT TERMS AND CONCEPTS

Be sure you can define or explain each of these terms before proceeding with the questions and problems.

independence of supply and demand
demand
demand schedule
demand curve
law of demand
quantity demanded
relative prices
shift or change in demand
substitute goods
complementary goods
consumer tastes or preferences
market demand
elasticity
price elasticity of demand
point elasticity
arc elasticity
total revenue

income elasticity
normal goods
inferior goods
supply
quantity supplied
shift or change in supply
technological change
elasticity of supply
excess supply
excess demand
equilibrium price
interdependence of markets
general equilibrium

Appendix:

cross elasticity

MULTIPLE-CHOICE QUESTIONS

Circle the letter corresponding with the most appropriate answer for each question.

1. The demand for eggs will not change, *ceteris paribus*, if there is:

   (a) a change in the price of eggs
   (b) a change in consumers' preference for eggs
   (c) an increase in consumer incomes
   (d) a change in the price of meat

2. As the price of a good increases from $1.50 to $2.00, the quantity demanded of the good falls from 45 to 25 units. The elasticity of demand for this good is:

    (a) 0.5
    (b) 1.0
    (c) 2.0
    (d) 2.5

3. When the percentage change in the quantity demanded is less than the percentage change in the price of that commodity, demand is:

    (a) elastic
    (b) inelastic
    (c) perfectly elastic
    (d) of unitary elasticity

4. When the demand for a good is quite elastic, one can reasonably assume that:

    (a) there are no close substitutes for the good
    (b) there are close substitutes for the good
    (c) the total expenditure for the good will not change when its price rises
    (d) there are no complementary goods for the good in question

5. Suppose the statistics show that Edmonton consumers bought 100,000 dozen eggs last week at $1.50 per dozen. One could infer from this data that:

    (a) the egg market in Edmonton was in equilibrium at a price of $1.50 per dozen
    (b) the demand for eggs is inelastic with respect to price
    (c) if there is no change in the price of eggs, there will be 100,000 dozen purchased again this week
    (d) none of the above is necessarily true

6. When an increase in the price of a commodity results in a decrease in the total revenue, we can conclude that:

    (a) demand is inelastic
    (b) demand is of unitary elasticity
    (c) demand is elastic
    (d) none of the above

7. If there is a major increase in the price of coffee—for which tea is regarded as a close substitute—one can reasonably expect that:

   (a) the demand for tea will decrease
   (b) the quantity of tea demanded will decrease
   (c) the demand for tea will increase
   (d) the quantity of tea demanded will not change

8. An increase in the wage rates for agricultural workers would cause the supply curve for potatoes to:

   (a) shift upward
   (b) shift downward
   (c) remain constant
   (d) slope downward to the right

9. An "increase in supply" refers to:

   (a) a rightward shift of the supply curve
   (b) a leftward shift of the supply curve
   (c) a movement upward along the supply curve
   (d) a movement downward along the supply curve

10. The price of a good increases from $10 to $12 and as a result the quantity supplied increases from 50 to 60 units. One can conclude that:

    (a) the supply is elastic
    (b) the supply is inelastic
    (c) the supply is of unitary elasticity
    (d) elasticity cannot be calculated since demand may have changed also

11. When the quantity demanded of a good is greater than the quantity supplied at a particular price, we would expect:

    (a) the price to fall
    (b) the price to rise
    (c) the supply curve to shift leftward
    (d) the demand curve to shift leftward

12. Which of the following statements is *incorrect*?

    (a) if supply increases and demand decreases, equilibrium price will fall
    (b) if supply decreases and demand remains constant, equilibrium price will rise
    (c) if demand decreases and supply increases, equilibrium price will rise
    (d) if demand increases and supply decreases, equilibrium price will rise

13. An increase in the supply of a commodity is likely the result of:

   (a) an increase in its selling price
   (b) a reduction in the price of inputs used to produce the good
   (c) an increase in the demand for the commodity
   (d) all of the above

14. Normal goods:

   (a) are not luxuries
   (b) have an income elasticity of less than 1.0
   (c) always have a price elasticity greater than 1.0
   (d) have an income elasticity greater than zero

Appendix:

15. The cross elasticity for two commodities that are close substitutes will be:

   (a) greater than zero
   (b) less than zero
   (c) less than if the commodities are complements
   (d) equal to zero

TRUE/FALSE QUESTIONS

State whether each of the following statements is true or false, or whether you are uncertain because the statement may be either true or false depending on the relevant circumstances and/or assumptions. Explain the reasons for your answer in each case.

1. If the price of chocolate increased by 10 per cent during the past year, yet the quantity of chocolate consumed fell by 15 per cent, we can conclude that the demand for chocolate is elastic.

2. When supply increases, the elasticity of supply at any price will decrease.

3. All demand curves intersect the quantity axis.

4. All supply curves intersect the quantity axis.

5. If there were an increase in income for each person, the demand for each commodity would increase.

6. If the price of eggs increases at the same time that consumers' incomes are increasing, the quantity of eggs purchased will increase.

7. When the demand for a commodity is inelastic, an increase in its price will cause the total revenue to increase.

Appendix:

8. A straight-line demand curve may be inelastic over its entire length.

9. The coefficient of supply elasticity changes over the length of a straight-line supply curve.

10. Inferior goods are those with a cross elasticity less than zero.

PROBLEMS

1. Assume the following information about the market for apples:

Price ($ per box)	0	4	6	8	10	12	16	20
Quantity demanded*	100	80	70	60	50	40	20	0
Quantity supplied*	0	0	0	13	27	40	67	93

*(thousands of boxes per week)

(a) Plot the information given above and join the points to draw the demand and supply curves in Figure 3.1.

Figure 3.1

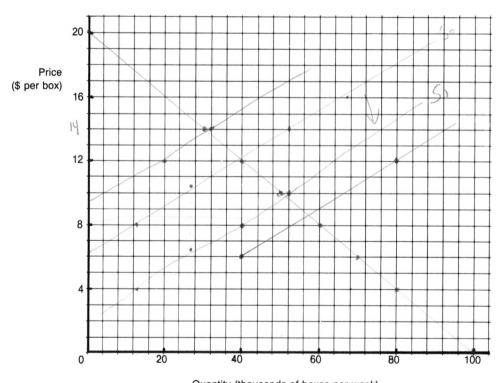

Quantity (thousands of boxes per week)

(b) What is the equilibrium price? _____ What is the quantity of apples exchanged (bought and sold) at this price? _____

(c) For each price *interval*, calculate the arc elasticity of supply and of demand.

Price: 0   4   6   8   10   12   16   20

Demand elasticity: —— —— —— —— —— —— ——

Supply elasticity: —— —— —— —— —— —— ——

(d) As the price falls, the slope of the demand curve will (increase/ decrease/remain constant). As the price falls, the elasticity of demand will (decrease/increase/remain constant).

(e) At what price would elasticity of demand be unitary? ——; perfectly elastic? ——; perfectly inelastic? ——. (Estimate these answers by referring to the elasticity coefficients calculated in (c) above.)

(f) Now assume that there is a change in technology such that at prices of $6 or more the quantity supplied would be 40,000 boxes more than is shown in the original supply schedule. Assume also that there is no change in demand. Plot the new supply curve on the graph and label it. The new equilibrium price would be $—— and the quantity exchanged would be ——boxes.

(g) Calculate the total revenue to suppliers at the original equilibrium price: ——; and at the new equilibrium price: ——.

(h) At a price of $12 per box, is the elasticity of the new supply curve greater or less than that of the original supply curve? ——. Will an outward parallel shift of the supply or demand curves always have this same general effect on elasticity at any given price? ——. Explain why.

_____

_____

_____

(i) Next, assume that *instead* of the technological change in (f) there is an increase in the price of fertilizers and sprays used in the apple orchards, such that the quantity supplied would be 20,000 boxes less than is shown at each price in the original supply schedule.

Plot the resulting supply curve and label it. The resulting equilibrium price would be $——, and the quantity exchanged would be ——.

2. Consider the effects of each of the following events on the market for beef consumed in Canada. Indicate by placing a +, -, or 0 under the appropriate heading whether there will be an increase, decrease, or no change in demand, supply, equilibrium price, and quantity exchanged.

Event	Demand	Supply	Price	Quantity Exchange
(a) Cholesterol in beef is increasingly believed to be the cause of heart attack	_____	_____	_____	_____
(b) Improved cattle feeds reduce beef production costs	_____	_____	_____	_____
(c) Pork sales are banned due to an outbreak of hog cholera	_____	_____	_____	_____
(d) The price of pork chops increases because government removes its subsidy for pork producers	_____	_____	_____	_____
(e) Canadian consumer incomes rise sharply as a result of decreased income taxes	_____	_____	_____	_____
(f) The price of cattle feed rises due to drought	_____	_____	_____	_____

QUESTIONS FOR REVIEW AND DISCUSSION

1. (a) Why are economists so interested in the equilibrium price of a commodity when the actual or observed price is often different from the equilibrium price?
   (b) What forces are at work to move the price of a commodity toward its equilibrium price?

2. List five commodities for which you think the demand is inelastic, and five for which the demand is elastic, over the range of prices usually observed for these commodities. Explain why the demand would be inelastic or elastic in each case.

3. Why is it incorrect to say that the demand for luxuries is elastic and the demand for necessities is inelastic? (Note that the chapter says "will tend to be more elastic or less inelastic" and question 2 above says "over the range of prices usually observed".)

4. List five pairs of commodities that are very close substitutes. Can you think of any *perfect* substitutes? If two commodities are perfect substitutes, are they in fact different commodities? List five pairs of commodities that are complementary goods. Are there any *perfect* complements?

5. Why is the price of salt so low even though it is so important for our physical health?

6. Use a supply and demand diagram to explain the probable changes in price and quantity purchased if the sale of marijuana were to be legalized and conducted without government controls.

4 Government in the Market Economy

IMPORTANT TERMS AND CONCEPTS

Be sure you can define or explain each of these terms before proceeding with the questions and problems.

"invisible hand"
market failure
imperfect competition
adjustment lags
barriers to markets
equitable income distribution
consumer sovereignty
floor prices
externalities
allocation
distribution

stabilization
public goods
exclusion principle
quasi-public goods
ceiling prices
black market
price controls
ad valorem tax
specific tax
subsidy

MULTIPLE-CHOICE QUESTIONS

Circle the letter corresponding with the most appropriate answer for each question.

1. Which of the following is *not* a basic criticism of the market system?

   (a) the market system limits personal freedom by imposing commodity prices that individual consumers cannot control
   (b) the market system does not take account of external costs and benefits
   (c) the market system sometimes adjusts slowly to changes in relative prices
   (d) the market system distributes income according to individuals' contributions to the economy (namely, the services of labour, land and capital) rather than according to individuals' needs

2. Negative externalities are:

   (a) decreases in the quality of goods or services
   (b) costs borne by society but not included in a firm's costs of production
   (c) the same as negative opportunity costs
   (d) factors that decrease the production-possibilities of an economy

3. The economic functions of government in a market system include:

   (a) stabilization of aggregate economic activity
   (b) equitable redistribution of income
   (c) reallocation of productive resources to more efficient uses
   (d) all of the above

4. A commodity is termed a pure "public good" if:

   (a) one person's consumption of the commodity does not exclude someone else from consuming the same commodity
   (b) one person's consumption of the commodity excludes someone else from consuming the same commodity
   (c) the majority of citizens want to consume that commodity
   (d) the market system can provide the commodity efficiently

5. Among the following commodities, the one most closely resembling a public good is:

   (a) automobiles
   (b) gasoline
   (c) towing services
   (d) highways

6. A price ceiling has an effect on the market only if:

   (a) it is greater than the equilibrium price
   (b) it is equal to the equilibrium price
   (c) it is less than the equilibrium price
   (d) no equilibrium price exists for that market

7. Rent controls tend to:

   (a) reduce the quantity of housing units supplied
   (b) increase the real income of renters relative to that of home-owners
   (c) be criticized by most economists
   (d) all of the above

8. A tax of 10¢ per unit will lead to an increase of 10¢ in the price of that good if:

   (a) the supply curve is downward-sloping
   (b) the demand is perfectly elastic
   (c) the demand is perfectly inelastic
   (d) none of the above

9. If a decrease in demand occurs at the same time that producers receive a subsidy, then in the new equilibrium:

   (a) quantity exchanged will always increase
   (b) both price and quantity will always decrease
   (c) the more elastic is the supply curve, the greater will be the decrease in price
   (d) none of the above

10. If pork producers receive a subsidy but beef producers do not:

   (a) the price of beef will rise
   (b) the price of beef will fall and the demand for beef will rise
   (c) the price of pork will fall because the supply increases
   (d) beef-eaters will derive no benefit from the subsidy to pork producers

11. Which of the following statements is *correct*?

   (a) if a ceiling price were imposed at a level below the equilibrium price, then the quantity demanded would be less than the quantity supplied
   (b) government imposition of a price ceiling must always result in the quantity demanded exceeding the quantity supplied
   (c) whenever there is excess demand in a market, one can expect an upward pressure on price
   (d) an equilibrium price and quantity will always be reached

12. Which of the following statements is *incorrect*?

   (a) given the supply curve, the more inelastic the demand for a product, the greater is the burden of a sales tax on consumers
   (b) if the demand for a good is inelastic, an increase in its price will result in an increase in total expenditure for that good
   (c) the higher a floor price is set above the equilibrium price, the greater will be the excess supply of that good
   (d) the further a ceiling price is below the equilibrium price, the smaller will be the excess demand or shortage of the good

13. A rent ceiling set below the equilibrium rent will:

    (a) increase the demand for housing units
    (b) increase the supply of housing units
    (c) increase the quantity demanded of housing units
    (d) all of the above

14. Many economists would propose, instead of rent controls:

    (a) legislation to increase land available for housing
    (b) grants to low-income families to assist with housing costs
    (c) removal of taxes on building materials
    (d) all of the above

15. The government's revenue from a sales tax will be greater:

    (a) the more elastic the demand for the good
    (b) the less elastic the demand for the good
    (c) if the good is a substitute instead of a complement
    (d) when a subsidy is offered for the substitute good

16. A floor price usually has no effect on:

    (a) the demand for a good
    (b) the supply of a good
    (c) either demand or supply of a good
    (d) all of the above

TRUE/FALSE QUESTIONS

State whether each of the following statements is true or false, or whether you are uncertain because the statement may be either true or false depending on the relevant circumstances and/or assumptions. Explain the reasons for your answer in each case.

1. The market system may provide controversial answers to the questions of What to produce? and For whom?, but there are no problems with its answers to How to produce?

2. Public goods are those that would not be produced except through collective action.

3. A government will raise more revenue from a specific tax on a commodity, the greater is the price elasticity of demand for the commodity.

4. When a tax of $.50 per unit is imposed on the sale of a commodity, the equilibrium price of the commodity will increase by $.50.

5. When a government imposes a floor price for a commodity, the equilibrium price will rise.

6. If the lagged adjustments in a market system could be overcome, a market could then take account of externalities.

7. An increase in the legal minimum wage may cause some unemployment, but at least the total income received by those still employed will increase.

8. Effective rent controls on all apartments in a metropolitan area would have a tendency to push up the price of houses in the area.

PROBLEMS

1. First, reproduce on Figure 4.1 the *original* supply and demand curves for apples that were plotted on Figure 3.1 in the previous chapter. (If you have not done that problem, use the information provided there to plot the curves directly on Figure 4.1 and then estimate the equilibrium price and the quantity exchanged.)

Figure 4.1

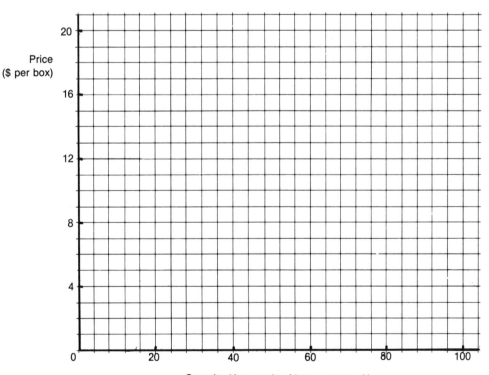

Quantity (thousands of boxes per week)

(a) Next, assume the government sets a floor price for apples of $14 per box. What will be the effect of the floor price legislation on the demand for apples? _____; on the supply of apples? _____. Will the apple suppliers' total revenue rise or fall as a result of the legislation? _____; by how much? _____. There will be a (shortage/surplus) of _____boxes of apples.

(b) Assume that under the original market conditions, the government instead decided to provide a subsidy of $4 per box to apple producers. Show the effect of the subsidy by plotting a new supply curve. What will be the new equilibrium price? _____and the quantity exchanged? _____. What will be the government's total subsidy payments to producers? _____. Will there be a shortage? _____ or surplus? _____. What would the total subsidy payments have been if the demand for apples were perfectly inelastic at a quantity of 40,000 boxes? _____, and if the demand were perfectly elastic at the original equilibrium price of $12 _____.

2. The curves D_1 and S_1 in Figure 4.2 show the market demand for and supply of a specific, routine medical service such as an annual physical examination, or treatment for a sore throat, skin rash, or sprained ankle.

Figure 4.2

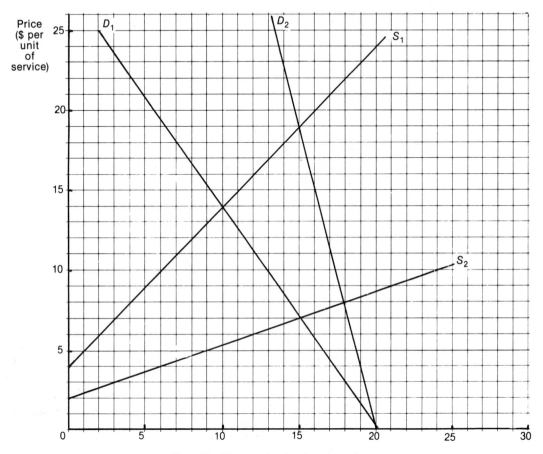

Quantity (thousands of units of service per month)

(a) The equilibrium price in this market is $_____$ per service with $_____$ units of service purchased per month. Total expenditure for this medical service is $_____$ per month.

(b) Suppose that the government recognizes external benefits associated with medical treatment (such as reduced employee absenteeism) and introduces a form of medicare that provides "free" medical service for everyone. (There are no charges and no premiums; the service is financed by payments to doctors from the government's general revenues.)

The most appropriate demand and supply curves to analyze this new situation will be _____ and _____ because _____

_____

_____

The new quantity demanded will be _____ units; medical doctors provide this service at a price of $_____ per unit, and the government finds that its total expenditure is $_____ per month.

(c) The government then decides to repeal "free" medicare and introduces a program whereby the government provides an income supplement or grant to be used only for medical care. This increases demand to D_2. The quantity now purchased is _____ at a price of $_____ per service, and the total expenditure for this medical service is $_____.

(d) Although the government was able to reduce its health expenditures by switching from the free medicare plan to the medical grant, it notes that the quantity purchased declined. The opposition critics argue that this is because the doctors increased their fees when the government announced the grant program; the critics therefore successfully press the government to control the doctors' fee schedule while maintaining the medical grant. The maximum fee that can then be charged for the medical service in question is set at $15. The result is that _____ units of this service are provided at a price of $_____ per unit. The total expenditure is now $_____.

(e) The doctors complain that their incomes have fallen, while the public complains that the doctors have reduced their office hours, that it is impossible to get an appointment within the next six weeks, and that there is a serious doctor shortage. A royal commission is appointed to study the problem. It recommends that the government maintain the grant, remove its ceiling on fees, establish new medical schools in the province, increase grants to medical students, encourage immigration of medical doctors from other countries, and introduce legislation giving supervised nurses the right to provide routine medical services previously restricted to doctors. The government implements all of these proposals.

Consequently, the supply increases to S_2, and the new equilibrium price is $_____ with a quantity of _____ units. This is a greater quantity than was provided under the grants program prior to fee controls, but the total expenditure is now $_____ per month, which is just slightly more than the $_____ spent for this service under the original market conditions.

3. Assume that the egg market is in equilibrium with the demand and supply as shown in Figure 4.3:

Figure 4.3

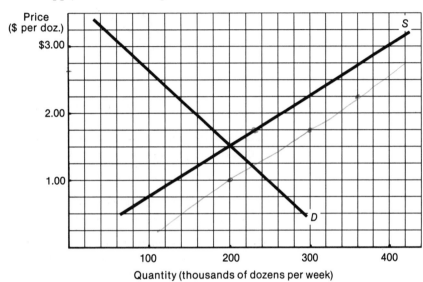

Price ($ per doz.)

Quantity (thousands of dozens per week)

(a) The equilibrium price is _____.
The output at this price is _____.
Elasticity of demand at the equilibrium price is (approx.) _____.
Elasticity of supply at the equilibrium price is _____.

(b) If the government offers a subsidy of $.50 per dozen, the new equilibrium price will be _____ and the output will be _____. The total cost of the subsidy to the government will be _____ per week.

(c) If the government imposes a quota (instead of the above program) whereby each producer is permitted to supply only an amount equal to one-half of the original output, the new price will be _____. The total revenue of egg producers will (increase/decrease) by comparison with their original revenue, by $_____. This indicates that the elasticity of demand between $1.50 and $2.60 is (elastic/inelastic). Confirm this by calculating the elasticity. _____.

4. Circle the correct answer or fill in the blank:

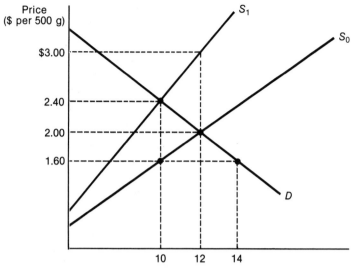

Price
($ per 500 g)

Quantity (thousands of units per week)

In the diagram above, assume that a tax has been imposed on butter, so that the supply curve shifts from S_0 to S_1.

(a) The original equilibrium price was _____.

(b) The tax apparently was a (specific/percentage) tax, set at ($_____ per unit/ _____% of the price).

(c) Over the price range from $2.00 to $2.40 the elasticity of demand for butter is _____; and the elasticity of supply is _____ between $2.40 and $3.00.

(d) As a result of the butter tax, one would expect the demand for margarine to (be unaffected/increase/decrease). The cross elasticity of butter and margarine likely would be (positive/negative/zero).

(e) If the demand were less elastic at $2.00, the increase in price resulting from the tax would be (greater than/equal to/less than) $.40.

(f) If a ceiling price were imposed at $1.60, what would be the result in terms of quantity supplied and quantity demanded, compared to the original equilibrium?

_____

_____

(g) What further action could government take to bring the market into equilibrium when it imposed ceiling price of $1.60?

_____

_____

_____

_____

_____

5. Suppose a study found that a subsidy for public transit (subways and buses) that reduces the fare by 10 per cent would increase the number of transit riders by 5 per cent in the first year, but by 15 per cent after two years.

   (a) What is the elasticity of demand in the first year? _____ and after two years? _____.

   (b) Why does the elasticity change during this time period?

   _____

   _____

   _____

   _____

   _____

QUESTIONS FOR REVIEW AND DISCUSSION

1. What did Adam Smith mean by "an invisible hand" and how was this expected to bring about the beneficial effects Smith mentions?

2. Outline the basic conditions that must exist for the market system to be of maximum benefit to consumers, that is, if the market is to be described as "perfect". Would there still remain a problem of "market failure"?

3. List as many instances as you can of external costs and of external benefits you have experienced today. What legislative or other changes might be made to bring these effects within the decision-making of persons who produced these effects?

4. Describe several examples of government intervention in the market system in Canada that produce better or worse results than you would expect to be produced in a pure market system. Think particularly of the basic economic decisions that were discussed in Chapter 1.

5. What conflicts are there among the three basic economic functions of government: allocation, distribution, and stabilization? Which of these functions should receive highest priority? Why?

6. Explain carefully why a government, rather than a private firm, might provide each of the following: traffic signals, weather forecasts, chest X-ray clinics, postal services.

7. Describe one example of each case where government uses taxes and subsidies to reallocate productive resources, and suggest reasons why such reallocations are thought to be socially desirable.

8. Do you agree with the book that ". . . the market system still responds by offering whatever consumers will buy"? Explain fully why you agree or disagree.

9. To what extent does "consumer sovereignty" have an effect on the automobile market? Consider specific changes in the product—such as size, comfort, safety, range of choice, and quality of materials—and indicate where consumers have influenced the suppliers as individual buyers, as associations, through government intervention, or not at all. Why has the consumer's influence been expressed in such diverse forms, again considering specific changes separately?

10. Suppose that effective rent-ceiling legislation were introduced but that any rental housing constructed in the following five years would be exempt. Use a supply-demand diagram to explain how this legislation would differ in its effect on prices and quantities from rent controls *without* such an exemption.

PART TWO

The Canadian Economy

5 Measuring Canada's Economic Performance

IMPORTANT TERMS AND CONCEPTS

Be sure you can define or explain each of these terms before proceeding with the questions and problems.

economic goals
inflation
demand-pull inflation
cost-push inflation
consumer price index (CPI)
base year
full employment
unemployment
unemployment rate
inadequate-demand unemployment
frictional unemployment
seasonal unemployment
structural unemployment
underemployment
labour force
seasonal adjustment
economic growth
labour productivity

households
firms
value added
Gross Domestic Product
Gross National Product
Net Domestic Income
indirect taxes
depreciation
Personal Income
transfer payments
Personal Disposable Income
investment (gross and net)
real income
GDP Price Index
GDP gap (or national income gap)
social indicators
underground economy

MULTIPLE-CHOICE QUESTIONS

Circle the letter corresponding with the most appropriate answer for each question.

1. Which of the following statements is *correct?*

   (a) inflation increases the real value of the Canadian dollar
   (b) inflation increases the real value of personal savings
   (c) inflation benefits creditors at the expense of debtors
   (d) inflation reduces the standard of living for persons on fixed incomes

2. "Full employment":

   (a) means that everyone has a job
   (b) is no longer a major economic goal in Canada
   (c) would be achieved when the unemployment rate is zero
   (d) is a concept that must be defined arbitrarily

3. If a wage increase of 5 per cent is accompanied by a 5 per cent increase in labour productivity:

   (a) this will result in inflation of 5 per cent
   (b) this should itself have no effect on inflation
   (c) workers' wages will actually rise by 10 per cent
   (d) producers' profit will fall by 5 per cent

4. If productivity increases faster in some industries than in others, the industry with the slower growth of productivity:

   (a) will not contribute to inflation
   (b) may contribute to inflation even if it does not raise the wages of its workers
   (c) may contribute to inflation if it provides wage increases equal to those in the industries with faster growth in productivity
   (d) may cause demand-pull inflation

5. An underlying cause of cost-push inflation is:

   (a) firms trying to increase profit margins
   (b) unions trying to raise wages by more than productivity increases
   (c) imperfections in the markets for goods and services
   (d) all of the above

6. Introducing training programs or reducing discriminatory hiring may serve to reduce primarily which type of unemployment?

   (a) frictional unemployment
   (b) structural unemployment
   (c) hidden unemployment
   (d) demand-deficient unemployment

7. Net Domestic Income includes all but which one of the following?

   (a) indirect taxes
   (b) corporate profits
   (c) interest and rental income
   (d) income of unincorporated enterprises

8. To compute Personal Income from Net Domestic Income, which of the following is *incorrect?*

    (a) deduct corporation income taxes
    (b) deduct corporation retained earnings
    (c) add government transfer payments
    (d) deduct depreciation (or capital cost allowance)

9. Which one of the following is *not* an investment item?

    (a) construction of a new school
    (b) purchase of a new canning machine by Campbell Soup Co.
    (c) purchase of 20 shares of Bell Canada stock
    (d) increase in unsold goods in Eaton's warehouses

10. Gross investment:

    (a) can never be less than zero
    (b) may be less than zero
    (c) is less than net investment
    (d) is included in Net Domestic Income

11. Net investment is negative if:

    (a) the economy is not expanding
    (b) imports exceed exports
    (c) nominal GDP increases by 6 per cent but prices increase by 8 per cent
    (d) depreciation (capital consumption allowance) is greater than gross investment

12. Net foreign investment is negative if:

    (a) the economy is not expanding
    (b) imports exceed exports
    (c) nominal GDP increases by 6 per cent but prices increase by 8 per cent
    (d) depreciation (capital consumption allowance) is greater than gross investment

13. GDP in current prices in 1986 was $505 billion; in 1990 it was $678 billion. The GDP implicit price index in 1986 was 100 and in 1990 it was 118.8. Between 1986 and 1990, the real GDP rose by about:

    (a) 3 per cent
    (b) 13 per cent
    (c) 23 per cent
    (d) 43 per cent

14. Government transfer payments are included in:

    (a) Gross Domestic Product
    (b) Personal Income
    (c) Domestic Income
    (d) Government purchases of goods and services

15. Comparisons of real GDP per capita between countries like Canada and India are difficult because Canada's GDP tends to be over-estimated relative to India's GDP, due to the fact that:

    (a) the average family size is higher in India
    (b) Canada has had a higher rate of inflation
    (c) India has a lower level of investment per capita
    (d) a higher percentage of economic activity in India does not involve monetary transactions

16. Suppose that the Canadian GDP for 1981 was $365 billion. One could therefore reasonably estimate that the GDP at exactly 12 noon, June 30, 1981 was:

    (a) $182.5 billion
    (b) $1 billion
    (c) $0.5 billion
    (d) not possible to calculate (undefined)

TRUE/FALSE QUESTIONS

State whether each of the following statements is true or false, or whether you are uncertain because the statement may be either true or false depending on the relevant circumstances and/or assumptions. Explain the reasons for your answer in each case.

1. Inflation at a lower rate than had been expected would benefit creditors more than debtors.

2. The CPI provides a better measure of changes in the cost of living for most college students than it does for their parents.

3. Cost-push inflation is more likely to occur when there is not much competition in labour markets and product markets.

4. Cost-push inflation always occurs when wage rates rise faster than improvements in labour productivity.

5. Total "value added" must logically be equal to the value of final goods and services.

6. Estimates of the annual GDP for Canada can be obtained by using either the incomes approach or the expenditures approach, because consumption spending is included in each approach.

7. The difference between GNE (or GNP) and GDP is that the former includes investment income but the latter does not.

8. Personal Income includes items other than wages and salaries.

9. Gross investment is greater than net investment.

PROBLEMS

1. Only some of the national accounts data are available for three different economies. Using these data and your knowledge of the component categories of the various accounts, calculate the missing data.

		Economy	
Item	A	B	C
Gross domestic product	300	200	155
Net domestic income	260	180	145
Personal income	225	145	135
Personal disposable income	175	125	120
Indirect taxes	15	10	5
Undistributed corporate profits	20	15	5
Net investment	75	40	35
Government expenditure on goods and services	40	35	20
Depreciation	25	10	5
Corporate income tax	20	20	10
Personal consumption	160	115	95
Personal income taxes	50	20	15
Government transfer payments	5	0	5
Personal saving	15	10	25
Exports	30	20	10
Imports	30	20	10
Subsidies	0	0	0

2. Indicate by writing I, E, or N beside each item whether it is included in the income side or the expenditure side of GDP, or neither of these accounts:

   __I__ (a) interest payment received by holder of a corporation's bond
   __E__ (b) purchase of a new boat for cod fishing
   __N__ (c) purchase of 50 acres by a farmer
   __N__ (d) government grant to a college student
   __N__ (e) purchase of a used van by a delivery service
   __E__ (f) increase in a pencil producer's inventory at year-end
   __E__ (g) government's payments for highway construction
   __I__ (h) salary and commission received by a salesperson
   __I__ (i) tips received by a bell-hop
   __N__ (j) purchase of a Tom Thomson painting (dated 1915) by a public art gallery
   __I__ (k) net income received by Canadian artist Robert Bateman for his paintings
   _____ (l) receipts from the sale of Canadian-made auto parts to the United States

3. Can gross investment ever be negative? _____ Why? _____

   _____

   Can net investment be negative if gross investment is positive? _____

   Why? _____

   _____

4. (a) Compute the missing data in the following table:

Year	Money GDP (GDP in current prices) (billions)	GDP Price Index	Real GDP (billions)	Population (millions)	Real GDP per Capita
1982	$374.4	87.9	$426.0	24.5	$17 387
1985	$478.0	97.6	$489.8	25.2	$51,454.419 43/
1989	$651.6	115.2	$565.7	26.2	$21,590

   (b) Money GDP increased by __27.7__ per cent from ~~1979~~ 1982 to ~~1985~~ 1989, but real GDP increased by __19__ per cent. The average annual rate of increase in money GDP in this period was __9.2__ per cent, while for real GDP it was __5__ per cent.

5. What difficulties or shortcomings are there in using the Consumer Price Index for Canada as a measure of the change in the cost of living for a typical student at the University of Saskatchewan?

_____

_____

_____

_____

QUESTIONS FOR REVIEW AND DISCUSSION

1. Explain why comparisons of GDP over time or among countries should be regarded only as imprecise estimates.

2. In the national income accounts, should the expenditures for a college education be treated as consumption or investment? Why?

3. "Inflation is a much more serious problem than unemployment because inflation affects everyone while unemployment is a problem only for those out of work." Do you agree? Why?

4. Would you regard the high unemployment rate for young people (aged 19 to 24) to be due mainly to frictional, seasonal, cyclical, or structural unemployment? Why?

5. Which of the five basic economic goals do you think should receive highest priority in the federal government's economic policy? Why?

6. Why are real estate assets said to be a "hedge against inflation"?

7. What is the difference between "income" and "wealth"? (Explain in terms of stocks and flows.)

8. Why is it necessary to remove government transfer payments from total government expenditures before estimating GDP? Why do private transfer payments (or gifts) not appear as a separate item in the national income accounts?

9. What is the difference between net investment and net foreign investment?

10. When is a bag of flour an intermediate good, and when is it a final good, for purposes of national income accounting? Why does this difference exist?

11. "Although the nominal GDP rose by 10 per cent last year this does not mean that Canadians are 10 per cent better off". Give specific reasons why you agree or disagree.

12. Why would GDP not provide an adequate comparison of the standard of living in different countries? Explain how you would interpret "standard of living". How would you modify the national income accounts to provide better international comparisons of standards of living?

6 Aggregate Expenditure and National Income

IMPORTANT TERMS AND CONCEPTS

Be sure you can define or explain each of these terms before proceeding with the questions and problems.

laissez-faire
Say's law
Keynesian revolution
aggregate expenditure
consumption (domestic vs. total)
saving
investment
propensity to consume
propensity to save
propensity to import
average vs. marginal propensity
shift in aggregate expenditure
expected yield
marginal efficiency of investment
investment demand
government spending
exports
domestic output

equality line
equilibrium national income
unplanned inventories
planned injections
planned withdrawals
multiplier
balanced budget multiplier
foreign trade multiplier
paradox of thrift
accelerator (acceleration principle)
inflationary gap
deflationary gap
national income gap
aggregate demand
aggregate supply
general price level
output vs. input prices

MULTIPLE-CHOICE QUESTIONS

Circle the letter corresponding with the most appropriate answer for each question.

1. A basic assumption in the classical economists' view of national income determination was that:

   (a) improved technology would keep the economy growing
   (b) wages, prices, and interest rates could rise or fall readily in response to changing economic conditions
   (c) government intervention would keep unemployment at a low level
   (d) enough money would be printed to make sure that demand would be equal to supply

2. Say's Law states that:

   (a) prices are always flexible
   (b) demand creates its own supply
   (c) an economy must always return to full employment
   (d) none of the above

3. Which of the following statements is *incorrect?*

   (a) savings represent the postponing of consumption
   (b) consumption depends primarily on the level of current disposable income
   (c) marginal propensity to consume is the share of total income that is used for consumption spending
   (d) investment includes new plant and equipment, new residential housing, new real additions to inventories

4. Government spending, as a component of aggregate expenditure:

   (a) includes only federal government expenditures
   (b) includes government transfer payments
   (c) excludes government transfer payments
   (d) has no direct effect on the level of national income

5. If the consumption curve shifts upward while the imports curve and tax rates remain constant, the saving curve must:

   (a) shift upward
   (b) shift downward
   (c) also remain constant
   (d) shift either upward or downward depending on the income level

6. The typical propensity to consume is one where:

   (a) MPC rises as income increases
   (b) APC declines as income increases
   (c) there is no dissaving, even at low incomes
   (d) there is a constant MPC

7. An economy is at its equilibrium level of national income when:

   (a) there is neither inflation nor unemployment
   (b) no output remains unsold
   (c) actual aggregate expenditure is equal to domestic output
   (d) planned aggregate expenditure is equal to domestic output

8. If an economy is temporarily not at the equilibrium level of national income, it will tend to move toward equilibrium because:

   (a) investment must equal saving
   (b) producers will not tolerate undesired increases or decreases in inventories
   (c) governments will adjust their budgets to bring the economy to equilibrium
   (d) the money supply will adjust to the equilibrium income level

9. If national income and output are being produced at the rate of $90 billion and planned aggregate expenditure is at the rate of $80 billion, then:

   (a) the economy is in equilibrium because income equals output
   (b) inventories are being depleted and income and output will rise
   (c) inventories are piling up and income and output will fall
   (d) inventories are being depleted and therefore aggregate expenditure will rise

10. When investment is assumed to be autonomous, this means that:

    (a) investment is not included in aggregate expenditure
    (b) investment is not determined by the level of GDP
    (c) the level of investment must remain constant
    (d) none of the above are true

11. An increase in national income can be expected to follow an increase in:

    (a) imports
    (b) tax revenues
    (c) government expenditures on goods and services
    (d) interest rates

12. A fall in national income can be expected to follow from an increase in:

    (a) consumption of domestic goods
    (b) personal income taxes
    (c) exports
    (d) residential construction

13. When the MPC is 0.9, the value of the multiplier is:

    (a) 0.9
    (b) 0.1
    (c) 1.0
    (d) 10.0

14. If every increase in GDP were accompanied by an equal increase in consumption spending, the multiplier would be equal to:

    $$\frac{1}{1-mpc}$$

    (a) zero
    (b) one
    (c) infinity
    (d) a value that cannot be calculated from the data supplied

15. If the marginal propensity to consume is 0.7, increases of $10 million in government expenditures and $10 million in income tax revenues:

    (a) will leave national income unchanged
    (b) will increase national income by $10 million
    (c) will increase national income by $7 million
    (d) will increase national income by $20 million

16. The "balanced-budget multiplier" refers to a special case of the multiplier in which:

    (a) the government has a balanced budget
    (b) the change in government expenditures is equal to the change in tax revenues
    (c) the economy is in equilibrium at the full-employment level
    (d) transfer payments are included in government spending

17. According to the Paradox of Thrift, if most families in the economy attempt to increase their saving at the same time:

    (a) aggregate expenditure will decline and total saving will increase
    (b) aggregate expenditure will decline and total saving will not increase
    (c) aggregate expenditure will increase and total saving will not increase
    (d) aggregate expenditure will increase and total saving will increase

18. The acceleration principle:

    (a) defines the effect of an autonomous increase in investment spending on the level of national income
    (b) specifies the percentage change in investment that will occur with each 1 per cent change in consumption
    (c) assumes that firms are operating at full capacity and expects that increases in sales are not temporary, and that the supply of investment goods is highly elastic
    (d) assumes that increases in consumption are dependent on increases in investment

19. In the simple Keynesian model, an economy will experience inflation at the full-employment level of national income if:

    (a) domestic output exceeds planned aggregate expenditure
    (b) domestic output is equal to planned aggregate expenditure
    (c) the value of the multiplier is less than one
    (d) domestic output is less than planned aggregate expenditure

20. The aggregate demand curve would shift outward if there were:

    (a) a decrease in the general level of prices
    (b) an outward shift of the aggregate supply curve
    (c) a decrease in personal income taxes
    (d) a decrease in input prices

21. The aggregate supply curve would shift outward if there were:

    (a) a decrease in the general level of prices
    (b) an outward shift of the aggregate demand curve
    (c) a decrease in personal income taxes
    (d) a decrease in input prices

TRUE/FALSE QUESTIONS

State whether each of the following statements is true or false, or whether you are uncertain because the statement may be either true or false depending on the relevant circumstances and/or assumptions. Explain the reasons for your answer in each case.

1. "Supply creates its own demand."

2. A reduction in corporate income tax rates would likely shift the *MEI* curve upward.

3. An increase in national income usually causes an increase in autonomous investment.

4. An increase in desired saving will likely cause a decrease in national income.

5. Undesired or insufficient inventories are a major factor leading an economy toward equilibrium national income.

6. An economy can be in equilibrium only at the full-employment level of national income.

7. The aggregate demand curve represents the planned aggregate expenditure that would occur at each price level.

8. The higher the general level of prices, the lower will be the equilibrium level of real national income.

9. Aggregate supply is the total output of final goods and services offered at each level of output prices, given the level of input prices.

PROBLEMS

1. The diagram below is for an economy where there is no government and no foreign trade, and investment spending is zero.

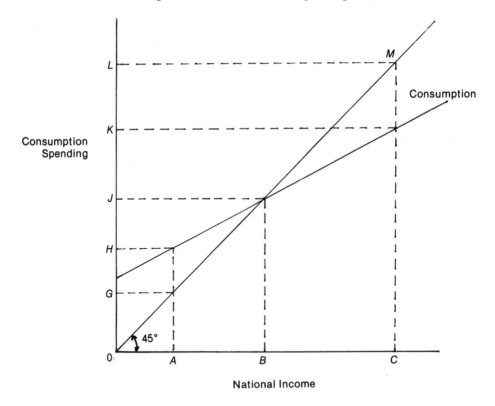

(a) The average propensity to consume in this economy is always (greater than/equal to/less than) the marginal propensity to consume, but the *APC* (increases/remains constant/decreases) as national income increases, while the *MPC* (increases/remains constant/decreases). The *MPC* at income 0*A* is equal to *JH/AB*; at income 0*C* the *MPC* is equal to _____ or _____.

(b) The economy is dissaving an amount equal to _____ at income 0*A* and continues dissaving until is reaches income 0*B*. Here, saving is equal to _____; at income 0*C* saving is equal to _____.

(c) The marginal propensity to save at income level 0*B* is (negative/zero/positive), and is equal to _____.

(d) If consumption spending were increased at each income level by an amount equal to *KL*, show how this would affect the consumption curve, by drawing the new curve on the graph above.

   As a result of this shift, the *MPC* at income level 0*C* is equal to _____, and the *APC* at income 0*C* is equal to _____. Hence, the *MPC* has (increased/decreased/remained constant) and the *APC* has (increased/decreased/remained constant).

(e) Now assume that instead of the consumption shift in (d) there is investment in the economy that is equal to *KL* and is constant for all levels of income. The *MPC* now is (greater than/the same as/less than) the *MPC* calculated in (a). The new equilibrium national income is equal to _____.

2. Assume that you have the following information for an economy, in terms of billions of dollars:

Y:	50	60	70	80	90	100
C:	40	49	57	64	70	75
AE:	56	65	73	80	86	91
MPC:	0.9	0.8	0.7	0.6	0.5	
Multiplier:	10	5	3.3	2.5	2	

where *Y* is GDP and *C* is domestic consumption, and planned investment, government spending, and net exports are exogenous, or autonomous: $I = 8$, $G = 5$, $(X - M) = 3$.

(a) In the table above, calculate aggregate expenditure (*AE*) for each level of *Y*. Calculate the *MPC* and the value of the multiplier for each interval in the national income and insert these values in the spaces between income levels in the table above.

(b) What is the equilibrium level of national income? $_____. If the economy were temporarily at an income level of $90 billion, what would be the amount of unplanned inventory change? $_____. Estimate the value of the multiplier *at* the equilibrium national income: _____.

(c) Assume that planned investment spending increases autonomously by $1 billion when the national income is at its equilibrium level. Approximately what will be the new equilibrium level of national income? _____. What approximately will be the new level of consumption? _____.

(d) If the full-employment level of national income is $90 billion, by how much must aggregate expenditure be increased to move the economy from its original equilibrium to full employment equilibrium? _____.

3. Suppose that an economy is in equilibrium with national income at $300 billion. If full-employment national income is estimated to be $360 billion and the marginal propensity to consume is 0.8:

(a) What is the value of the multiplier? _____.

(b) What is the GDP gap? _____; and the deflationary gap? _____.

(c) What increase in desired aggregate expenditure is required to close the gap? _____.

(d) Would an increase in government tax revenue and expenditure of $12 billion close the gap? _____. Why? _____

_____

(e) Would an increase in government expenditures of $12 billion (with taxes unchanged) close the gap? _____. Why?_____

_____

_____

4. Assume that an economy is at its equilibrium national income. Then state and explain the effect on national income of each of the following:

(a) tax rates are increased.

(b) there is an increase in the average propensity to consume.

(c) there is an autonomous increase in government spending.

5. Suppose that an economy has the aggregate expenditure function shown in the diagram below. Full-employment income is 400.

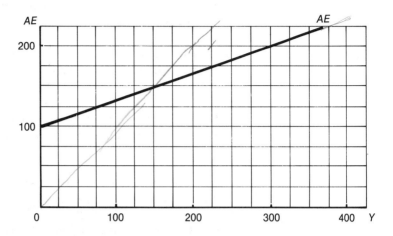

(a) What is the equilibrium level of national income (Y) in this economy? _____.

(b) What is the value of the multiplier? _____.

(c) If aggregate output is 200, unintended inventories will be _____.

(d) Show how a decrease in the marginal tax rates on personal income would affect aggregate expenditure, by drawing a new AE_1 curve.

(e) By how much would government spending have to increase for this economy to achieve full employment? _____.

QUESTIONS FOR REVIEW AND DISCUSSION

1. What logical connection(s) is (are) there between the way the term "investment" is used in economics and the way this word is used in the world of financial affairs?

2. What is the difference between autonomous investment and induced investment? How does an autonomous increase in investment affect GDP?

3. Explain carefully the difference between a shift in the *MEI* curve and a movement along this curve, and outline the factors that cause each of these changes.

4. Explain why the domestic output curve is shown as a 45° line, when the scales on both axes are the same.

5. Why is the value of the multiplier calculated from the marginal propensity to consume rather than from the average propensity to consume?

6. "If the marginal propensity to consume were always equal to one, for all persons at all times, there would be no equilibrium level of national income." Do you agree? Explain.

7. Consider how the accelerator principle can be used to explain (and predict) the boom in school construction and the teacher shortage of the 1955-65 period compared with the closing of schools and the teacher surplus in the 1975–1985 period?

8. Which industries do you think would show the strongest influence of the acceleration principle? Explain carefully.

7 Money and Banking in Canada

IMPORTANT TERMS AND CONCEPTS

Be sure you can define or explain each of these terms before proceeding with the questions and problems.

money
functions of money
characteristics of money
barter
goldsmith receipts
legal tender
money supply
near-money
banking system
financial system
chartered banks
central bank
Bank of Canada

balance sheets
chartered bank assets, liabilities
treasury bill
"lender of last resort"
cash reserves
excess reserves
desired reserves
reserve ratio
Bank Rate
deposit expansion and
    contraction
open market operations
moral suasion

MULTIPLE-CHOICE QUESTIONS

Circle the letter corresponding with the most appropriate answer for each question.

1. The narrow (M1) definition of the money supply includes:

   (a) coins only
   (b) coins and paper currency only
   (c) coins and paper currency in circulation and demand deposits at the chartered banks
   (d) coins and paper currency in circulation and all bank deposits

2. The major component of the narrowly-defined money supply is:

   (a) coins
   (b) paper currency
   (c) demand deposits
   (d) government deposits

3. The chartered banks receive their charters from:

   (a) the Bank of Canada
   (b) the Parliament of Canada
   (c) the Minister of Finance
   (d) the provincial governments

4. Treasury bills are short-term bonds representing a debt incurred by:

   (a) the Bank of Canada
   (b) the Government of Canada
   (c) a chartered bank
   (d) a finance company

5. When chartered banks have made loans to the maximum possible total amount, given their desired reserve ratio, they will have:

   (a) no excess reserves
   (b) no currency reserves
   (c) no reserves
   (d) no cash reserves

6. Assume the total banking system has deposits of $50 billion and reserves of $8.5 billion. If the desired reserve ratio is 15 per cent, the banking system can expand the money supply by a maximum further amount of:

   (a) $6.67 billion
   (b) $7.50 billion
   (c) $8.50 billion
   (d) $1.00 billion

7. Which of the following would be included in the liabilities of a chartered bank's balance sheet?

   (a) Treasury Bills
   (b) reserves at the Bank of Canada
   (c) demand deposits
   (d) mortgage loans

8. When a chartered bank makes a loan, the first result is that:

   (a) the bank gives currency for the amount of the loan to the borrower
   (b) the bank gives a cheque for the amount of the loan to the borrower
   (c) the bank adds the amount of the loan to the balance in the borrower's chequing account at the bank
   (d) the bank adds the amount of the loan to the balance in the borrower's savings account at the bank

9. In terms of dollar amounts, the major part of the money supply is created by:

   (a) the Bank of Canada
   (b) the Government of Canada
   (c) the chartered banks
   (d) the Mint

10. The major purpose of chartered bank deposits at the Bank of Canada is to:

    (a) give the Bank of Canada funds that it can loan out as "lender of last resort"
    (b) provide the basis for inter-bank settlement of net balances
    (c) protect depositors by assuring that banks can meet the demands for cash
    (d) reduce the profits of the chartered banks

11. An increase in the desired cash reserve ratio:

    (a) increases the amount the banks can loan
    (b) decreases the amount the banks can loan
    (c) reduces the chartered bank balance at the central bank
    (d) increases the demand deposits banks may hold

12. If a bank sells a bond to the Bank of Canada for $100,000 and the desired reserve ratio is 10 per cent, this particular bank may initially increase its loans by:

    (a) $10,000
    (b) $90,000
    (c) $100,000
    (d) $1,000,000

13. Which of the following statements is *incorrect*?

    (a) when the Bank of Canada purchases bonds from the public, there will be an increase in the money supply
    (b) by changing the Bank Rate, the Bank of Canada can directly change the money supply
    (c) a restrictive monetary policy is intended to reduce the growth of aggregate expenditure
    (d) cash reserves include currency held by the chartered banks

TRUE/FALSE QUESTIONS

State whether each of the following statements is true or false, or whether you are uncertain because the statement may be either true or false depending on the relevant circumstances and/or assumptions. Explain the reasons for your answer in each case.

1. The M1 component of the money supply includes federal government deposits at the chartered banks.

2. The Bank of Canada can change the Bank Rate at any time.

3. If the Bank of Canada purchases government bonds from the chartered banks, the money supply will increase.

4. The Bank of Canada creates chartered bank reserves, but the chartered banks create money.

5. If the cash reserve ratio is 10 per cent, the money supply could be increased by a maximum of 10 times the initial increase in reserves. The actual increase may, however, be less than this.

6. Since there are about five times as many foreign banks as there are Canadian chartered banks now operating in Canada, it is likely that the foreign banks will soon do most of Canada's banking business.

PROBLEMS

1. For each of the following cases, show the *initial* changes in deposits, reserves, loans, or securities, in each balance sheet as in the example below. Show the changes in *excess* reserves in brackets below any entry for reserves. Assume that the desired reserve ratio is 10 per cent.

	Bank of Canada		Chartered Banks		Public	
	A	L	A	L	A	L
(a) You deposit a dirty $20 bill at your bank, which returns it to the Bank of Canada for disposal		res + 20 curr -20	res + 20 (ex.r. + 18)	dep + 20	dep + 20 curr -20	
(b) Your bank loans you $100		ex.r -90	loan +100 (ex.r. +90	dep +100 dep -100	dep+100	loans +100
(c) Bank of Canada buys a $1,000 bond from a chartered bank	Sec +1000	ex.res.- rest +1000	Sec -1000 (sales (-900) res. +1000 (ex.r +1000	dep +1000		
(d) You pay college fees of $400 by cheque; the college deposits this in its bank account			res -400 res +400	dep -400 dep +400	dep +100 dep -400 dep +400	
(e) Bank of Canada transfers $500 in Govt. of Canada deposits from the B. of C. to a chartered bank		dep -500 res +500	res +500 (ex.r. +450)	dep +500		

2. For each of the cases presented in question 1, show the *final accumulated changes* in each balance sheet as in the example below. Continue to assume that the reserve requirement is 10 per cent; and assume further that the public does not change its holdings of currency and that banks are able to loan all excess reserves.

	Bank of Canada		Chartered Banks		Public	
	A	L	A	L	A	L
(a) deposit of $20 bill		res + 20	res + 20	dep + 200	dep + 200	loans + 180
		curr -20	loans + 180		curr -20	
(b) loan of $100			loan +100			loan
(d) cheque to college is redeposited at same bank						
(e) transfer of Govt. of Can. deposits						

3. Assume that the Bank of Canada sells a $100,000 (or $100K) bond to an insurance company, which pays for the bond by drawing a cheque on its account at a chartered bank. Reserve requirement is 10 per cent.

(a) Show the *initial* changes of this transaction in the balance sheets below.

	Bank of Canada		Chartered Banks		Public	
	A	L	A	L	A	L

The chartered banks now have a reserve deficiency of $_____.

(b) The chartered banks may decide to return reserves to the desired level by borrowing from the Bank of Canada. The banks would need to borrow $_____. This would appear in the chartered banks' balance sheet on the assets side as _____ and on the liabilities side as _____. The assets entry for the Bank of Canada would be _____ and the liability entry would be _____. The *net* effect of this open-market transaction and Bank loan is that chartered bank reserves (rise/fall) by $_____. Demand deposits (rise/fall) by $_____ and the money supply is (increased/decreased) by $_____.

(c) If the chartered banks eliminate the reserves deficiency by reducing their loans to the public instead of borrowing from the Bank of Canada, the total decrease in loans will need to be $_____. This follows from the fact that the banks must reduce demand deposits by _____ if the existing reserves are to be sufficient to meet the desired reserve requirements. The final effect of the open-market transaction, if the banks take this second course of action, will be that chartered bank reserves have (fallen/risen) by $_____; demand deposits have (fallen/risen) by $_____; and the money supply has (increased/decreased) by $_____.

(d) Hence the (reserve borrowing/loan reduction) of the chartered banks has the stronger effect on the money supply.

(e) Suppose that after the foregoing changes have occurred, the chartered banks hold a total of $60 billion in deposits against which they hold cash reserves of 10 per cent. If the banks' desired reserve ratio increases to 11 per cent, the chartered banks will have a reserve deficiency of $_____.

(f) If at the same time the Bank of Canada raises the Bank Rate to discourage the chartered banks from borrowing the desired reserves from the Bank, the chartered banks will have to reduce loans to the public by $_____. This reduces demand deposits by $_____ and reduces the money supply by $_____.

QUESTIONS FOR REVIEW AND DISCUSSION

1. It is sometimes said that Canada will soon be a "cashless" society. What does this mean? Describe some of the changes that would be required to achieve a completely cashless society. What advantages and disadvantages would there be? Could Canada also become a "moneyless" society?

2. What happens to the level of the money supply when someone withdraws $500 in currency from his or her bank account for a vacation trip? Does it ultimately matter whether the trip is within Canada or another country? Why?

3. Why can one say that the banking system creates money if a bank is permitted to lend only part of its deposits?

4. What determines the quantity of coins and paper currency in circulation?

5. Suppose that chartered banks held cash reserves equal to 100 per cent of their deposits. Would this mean that the Bank of Canada could no longer have an influence on the money supply?

6. Bank of Canada actions to increase the money supply have been described as "trying to push on a string". Is this a valid analogy?

7. Why does money have value if there is nothing "backing" the money supply?

8. What is the difference between money and bonds? Is there any difference between money and gold? Explain.

8 Money and National Income

IMPORTANT TERMS AND CONCEPTS

Be sure you can define or explain each of these terms before proceeding with the questions and problems.

real sector
monetary sector
stock of money
quantity theory of money
velocity of money
income velocity of money
quantity equation of exchange
demand for money
transactions demand
liquidity preference

liquidity trap
supply of money
bond yield rate
equilibrium interest rate
inverse relationship of bond
    prices and yields

MULTIPLE-CHOICE QUESTIONS

Circle the letter corresponding with the most appropriate answer for each question.

1. One of the basic conclusions of classical economic theory was that:

    (a) any inflation would be temporary
    (b) any unemployment would be temporary
    (c) any real economic growth would be temporary
    (d) none of the above

2. The classical economists' crude quantity theory stated that in the short run an increase in the money supply would:

    (a) increase the quantity of real output
    (b) decrease the velocity of money
    (c) increase the average price level
    (d) have no effect on the economy

3. If there is an increase in the interest rate paid on savings accounts, there is likely to be:

(a) an increase in the demand for money
(b) an increase in the quantity of money demanded
(c) a decrease in the demand for money
(d) a decrease in the quantity of money demanded

4. The quantity of money demanded would likely increase if:

(a) interest rates were increasing and total spending was falling
(b) everyone were paid daily instead of once or twice a month
(c) interest rates were constant and total spending was increasing
(d) the supply of money was decreasing

5. According to Keynesian theory, an increase in the money supply has its effect on GDP through:

(a) changes in the velocity of money
(b) an increase in the demand for money and hence increased spending
(c) a lower interest rate and increased investment spending
(d) all of the above

6. An increase in the money supply may have little effect on the economy if:

(a) people do not understand why the money supply is increased
(b) there is an increase in the demand for money
(c) the interest rate falls at the same time
(d) the government has a budget deficit

7. A change in the interest rate generally has its strongest effect on:

(a) residential construction
(b) exports of manufactured goods
(c) construction of business plant and equipment
(d) government expenditures

8. Changes in the money supply may not have much effect on real GDP if:

(a) investment is highly responsive to changes in the interest rate
(b) the income velocity of money is constant
(c) investment is not very sensitive to changes in the interest rate
(d) the demand for money is constant

TRUE/FALSE QUESTIONS

State whether each of the following statements is true or false, or whether you are uncertain because the statement may be either true or false depending on the relevant circumstances and/or assumptions. Explain the reasons for your answer in each case.

1. With an increase in aggregate expenditure, and no change in the money supply, interest rates are likely to rise.

2. An increase in the rate of growth of the money supply will decrease the velocity of money.

3. When the price of a bond increases, its actual yield rate declines.

4. An increase in national income will likely increase the quantity of money actually held at any interest rate.

5. Increases in the money supply will have no effect on investment if investment is inelastic with respect to the interest rate.

PROBLEMS

1. Suppose that you are given the following data for an economy and assume that you are basing your answers to the following questions on the sophisticated quantity theory, using the income-velocity of money.

Given that M = 20,000
                  P = 100
                  Q = 600
                  V = a constant

(a) The velocity of circulation is _____.

(b) Assuming full employment exists, a 5 per cent increase in the money supply will result in _____

_____ .

(c) Suppose that technological improvements make it possible to achieve a real growth rate of 10 per cent annually. By how much could the money supply be increased without causing inflation? _____ .

If the money supply remained unchanged, the result would be

_____ .

2. Given the information portrayed in these diagrams:

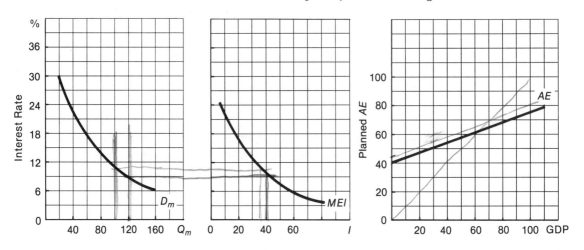

(a) Suppose that the money supply is increased from $100 billion to $120 billion. The resulting new interest rate would be _____ %.

(b) This change in the interest rate would be expected to lead to a(n) (increase/decrease) in investment of $_____ billion. From these results one can conclude that the elasticity of investment with respect to the interest rate is (elastic/unitary/inelastic) because the elasticity coefficient is _____. [Hint: recall the formula for price elasticity.]

(c) If there is no GDP-induced investment, the change in investment will (increase/decrease) planned aggregate expenditure by $_____ billion. The GDP will (increase/decrease) by $_____ billion. From this, one can conclude that the value of the multiplier is _____and the MPC is _____.

(Review carefully the assumptions that must hold true for each of these changes to occur, and particularly to result in the specific values that you have estimated in each case.)

QUESTIONS FOR REVIEW AND DISCUSSION

1. Does an increase in the money supply always cause inflation? Explain.

2. Why is the quantity equation of exchange necessarily true?

3. Discuss the several circumstances or conditions under which an increase in the money supply might have little or no effect on the level of employment.

4. "The Bank of Canada should try to maintain a stable interest rate in order to avoid inflation or unemployment." Do you agree? Why?

5. What is the difference between money and income? Between money and wealth?

6. Use the *AD-AS* diagram to explain why complementary monetary and fiscal policies (such as increasing both the money supply and government spending) will have a stronger impact on GDP than either policy taken separately.

9   Fiscal Policy and the Public Debt

IMPORTANT TERMS AND CONCEPTS

Be sure you can define or explain each of these terms before proceeding with the questions and problems.

stabilization policies   discretionary fiscal policy
fiscal policy   policy lags
monetary policy   recognition lag
Phillips curve or trade-off curve   budget deficit or surplus
natural rate of unemployment   functional finance
NAIRU   full-employment balance
"stagflation"   structural deficit
automatic stabilizers   public debt
fiscal drag   wealth effect

MULTIPLE-CHOICE QUESTIONS

Circle the letter corresponding with the most appropriate answer for each question.

1. If an economy were experiencing the short-run Phillips curve relationship between unemployment and inflation, fiscal and monetary policies to increase aggregate expenditure would:

   (a) reduce unemployment and increase inflation
   (b) increase unemployment and reduce inflation
   (c) increase unemployment and increase inflation
   (d) reduce unemployment and reduce inflation

2. The outward shift of the short-run Phillips curve is *least* likely to be caused by:

   (a) monopoly power of corporations and unions
   (b) consumer expectations of higher prices
   (c) geographical immobility of labour resources
   (d) neutral fiscal policy

3. Which of the following is *not* an example of a built-in stabilizer?

   (a) unemployment compensation
   (b) welfare programs
   (c) progressive personal income tax rates
   (d) expansionary fiscal policy

4. An increasing marginal propensity to save is an effective built-in stabilizer, because as national income increases:

   (a) the marginal propensity to consume increases
   (b) the marginal propensity to save decreases
   (c) a smaller fraction of additional income will go to consumption
   (d) a larger portion of income will go to consumption

5. The effect of a government's budget surplus on the equilibrium level of GDP is substantially the same as:

   (a) an increase in consumption
   (b) an increase in investment
   (c) an increase in saving
   (d) an increase in exports

6. By a "full-employment budget balance" economists mean that:

   (a) governments should balance their budgets to achieve full employment
   (b) an expansionary deficit budget should be designed such that the government will have a balanced budget when the economy reaches full employment
   (c) balanced budgets can lead to full employment but cannot reduce inflation
   (d) budgets that are balanced over the cycle will lead to full employment

7. The federal government would be more likely to borrow from the public rather than from the Bank of Canada:

   (a) if the unemployment rate was high and rising
   (b) if it wished to keep interest rates as low as possible
   (c) if the government wished to have only a modest increase in aggregate expenditure
   (d) if the government wished to decrease the public debt

8. Interest payments on the public debt:

   (a) have been a declining percentage of GDP since 1960
   (b) represent no burden to the economy because "we owe the debt to ourselves"
   (c) are an obligation incurred in previous years and are therefore not included in the governments' current budgets
   (d) redistribute income from taxpayers to bondholders

TRUE/FALSE QUESTIONS

State whether each of the following statements is true or false, or whether you are uncertain because the statement may be either true or false depending on the relevant circumstances and/or assumptions. Explain the reasons for your answer in each case.

1. The short-run Phillips curve relationship suggested that an increase in inflation would lead to an increase in unemployment.

2. A large public debt represents a financial burden on future generations, who will be required to repay the debt.

3. A federal government deficit will have a more expansionary effect on GDP if it is financed by borrowing from the Bank of Canada rather than from the chartered banks.

4. An expansionary fiscal policy could cause an increase in frictional unemployment.

PROBLEMS

1. Assume that the Adanac economy experienced the following combinations of inflation and unemployment during the years shown:

Year	Inflation (annual percentage increase in CPI)	Unemployment (average annual percentage unemployed)
1960	1.5	5.5
1962	0.5	7.5
1964	2.5	4.5
1966	3.5	3.5
1968	6.5	3.0

(a) Plot these data on the graph to show the Phillips curve or trade-off curve facing the Adanac economy in the 1960s.

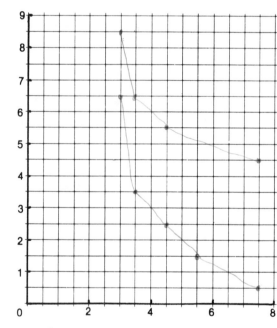

Average Annual Percentage Unemployed

(b) By the late 1970s the Adanac economy found that it was experiencing unemployment and inflation as follows:

Year	Inflation (%)	Unemployment (%)
1972	6.5	3.5
1974	8.5	3.0
1976	5.5	4.5
1978	4.5	7.5

Plot these data on the same graph to show the Phillips curve facing the Adanac economy in the 1970s. This indicates that there has been an outward shift in the Phillips curve and that the trade-off between unemployment and inflation is now different at any given level of inflation or unemployment. For example, in the 1960s, a three-percentage-point decrease in unemployment, from 7.5 to 4.5 per cent, would be accompanied by an increase in inflation from 0.5 to _____ per cent. But in the 1970s, with the economy at 7.5 per cent unemployment, a three-percentage-point decrease in unemployment would be accompanied by _____ per cent inflation, that is, an increase in the inflation rate of _____ percentage point(s).

(c) Fiscal and monetary policies are expected to (move the economy along the curve/shift the curve inward) by changing the level of (aggregate expenditure/inflation expectations).

(d) Labour supply programs and incomes policies are often proposed to (move the economy along the curve/shift the curve inward) on the assumption that these will reduce the (aggregate expenditure/structural/seasonal) problems of the economy.

2. Suppose an economy is at an equilibrium national income (GDP) level of $100 billion. At any income level, 75 per cent of additional GDP goes to consumption of domestic production. The estimated full-employment level of GDP is $112 billion. (Note: when $Y = 0$, $C = 0$.)

(a) Consumption is currently $_____ billion; the marginal propensity to consume is _____ and the value of the multiplier is _____.

(b) If fiscal policy is to be used to bring the economy to full-employment GDP, the government could change tax revenues, government spending, or both.

If government spending is to be changed while tax revenues remain constant, the government will need to (decrease/increase) its spending by $_____ billion.

If government spending is to remain constant while tax revenues are changed, these will need to (decrease/increase) by $_____ billion.

If the government's budget is now balanced and it wishes to maintain a balanced budget while achieving full-employment GDP, it will need to increase government spending and tax revenues by $_____ billion in each case.

QUESTIONS FOR REVIEW AND DISCUSSION

1. If a short-run Phillips curve represents an historical relationship between unemployment and inflation, which changes frequently, is the concept of a Phillips curve of any value in designing economic policy? Why do some economists argue that the long-run Phillips curve is vertical?

2. Why is the problem of time lags so important in setting fiscal policies?

3. Under what conditions would the federal government's budget deficit have little or no expansionary effect on the economy?

4. "It is not the existence of a large public debt, but rather the changes in the debt that have an influence on the economy." Do you agree? Why?

10 Monetary Policy and the Foreign Exchange Rate

IMPORTANT TERMS AND CONCEPTS

Be sure you can define or explain each of these terms before proceeding with the questions and problems.

asymmetry of monetary policy
investment inelasticity
income velocity
arbitrage
foreign exchange rates
foreign exchange markets
fixed or pegged exchange rates
floating or fluctuating exchange rates
Exchange Fund Account
foreign exchange reserves

Appendix:

gold standard
gold-exchange standard
two-tier system
special drawing rights (SDRs)
managed float
sliding pegged rates

MULTIPLE-CHOICE QUESTIONS

Circle the letter corresponding with the most appropriate answer for each question.

1. Monetary policy will be more effective in influencing the rates of inflation or unemployment if:

   (a) investment does not vary with interest rate changes
   (b) chartered banks have substantial excess reserves
   (c) the velocity of money does not change
   (d) the quantity of money people wish to hold does not depend on the interest rate

2. To say that the price of the Canadian dollar is $1.04 in terms of the American dollar is equivalent to saying that the price of the American dollar, in terms of the Canadian dollar, is:

   (a) $1.00
   (b) $0.96
   (c) $1.04
   (d) $0.925

3. The demand curve for Canadian dollars is downward sloping when plotted against the price of dollars in Swiss francs because:

   (a) an appreciation in the value of the dollar will cause the price of Canadian exports to fall in terms of Swiss francs
   (b) a depreciation in the value of the dollar will cause the price of Canadian exports to rise in terms of francs
   (c) when the dollar depreciates, the dollar price of Canadian exports to Swiss buyers will rise
   (d) none of the above

4. If Canada and the U.S. allow the foreign exchange rate of their currencies to float freely, a higher rate of inflation in Canada than in the U.S. will cause:

   (a) both the supply of and the demand for the Canadian dollar to increase
   (b) both the supply of and the demand for the Canadian dollar to decrease
   (c) the demand for the Canadian dollar to decrease and the supply to increase
   (d) the demand for the Canadian dollar to increase and the supply to decrease

5. In order to raise the foreign exchange rate of the Canadian dollar, the government (or the Bank of Canada) would be *least* likely to:

   (a) increase its foreign aid contributions
   (b) buy Canadian dollars on the foreign exchange market
   (c) restrict the number of dollars Canadian tourists could take to other countries
   (d) restrict imports

6. If the foreign exchange rate is fixed and an expansionary monetary policy is implemented:

   (a) there will be upward pressure on the foreign exchange rate
   (b) it will likely be necessary to sell foreign currencies from the Exchange Fund Account
   (c) this should correct any deficit in the balance of payments
   (d) it will be necessary to offset this with a contractionary fiscal policy

7. If an increase in the money supply lowers the Canadian rates relative to the interest rates in the United States:

   (a) this puts upward pressure on Canada's foreign exchange rate
   (b) this puts downward pressure on Canada's foreign exchange rate
   (c) this will have no effect on Canada's foreign exchange rate
   (d) this will result in Canada deciding to have a pegged exchange rate

8. During the period since 1950, Canada was on a fixed exchange rate for:

   (a) 2 years
   (b) 8 years
   (c) 16 years
   (d) 24 years

9. Canadian experience with monetary policy:

   (a) has shown that there is now too little co-ordination between the Bank of Canada and the Minister of Finance
   (b) has tended to include very few changes in the Bank Rate
   (c) has largely ignored the effect of interest rate changes on the foreign exchange rate
   (d) has changed from a passive reaction to economic conditions to a more aggressive use of the various tools of monetary policy

TRUE/FALSE QUESTIONS

State whether each of the following statements is true or false, or whether you are uncertain because the statement may be either true or false depending on the relevant circumstances and/or assumptions. Explain the reasons for your answer in each case.

1. When interest rates are rising, one can conclude that monetary policy is contractionary.

2. An increase in the money supply in Canada is likely to increase the supply of Canadian dollars in the foreign exchange market.

3. An advantage of monetary policy is that there are no lags associated with it.

4. Monetary policy is more effective if there is a high elasticity of investment with respect to interest rates.

5. Large holdings of near-money can offset much of the potential effect of a contractionary monetary policy.

6. The velocity of M1 money tends to increase during a period of expansionary monetary policy.

7. Monetary policy is intended to deal primarily with domestic problems such as inflation and unemployment.

8. Arbitrage refers to the buying of currency and then selling it later at a higher price.

9. The supply curve for domestic currency offered in exchange for a foreign currency is upward-sloping to the right.

10. When the exchange rate is pegged at an official level, it is the responsibility of the Bank of Canada to maintain this level.

11. The main advantage of a fixed exchange rate is that monetary policy can then be designed to deal only with domestic inflation.

12. Since putting the Canadian dollar on a floating system in 1970, the government has not had to intervene in the foreign exchange market.

13. Monetary policy in Canada has focused alternately on changes in the interest rate and changes in the supply of money.

PROBLEMS

1. Assume that a flexible exchange rate exists between Canada and Japan. Indicate by placing a +, −, or 0 under the appropriate heading whether there would be an increase, decrease, or no change in the demand, supply, equilibrium exchange rate, and quantity, of Canadian dollars exchanged for Japanese yen, in the short-run.

Event	Demand for C$	Supply of C$	Exchange Rate, Yen per $1.00	Quantity of C$
(a) Japanese buy fewer shares in a Canadian corporation	−	0	−	−
(b) Inflation occurs at a higher rate in Japan than in Canada	+	−	+	?
(c) Japan has a sharp increase in its rate of real economic growth	+	0	+	+
(d) There is a substantial decrease in the number of tourist-days that Japanese spend in Canada	−	0	−	−

2. From the following data, draw the supply and demand curves for the Canadian dollar on the graph provided to represent the foreign exchange market for dollars and British pounds (£).

Price of C$ in £	Quantity Demanded (per month)	Quantity Supplied (per month)
	(millions of C$)	
£.35	48,500	28,000
.38	45,800	30,500
.41	43,100	33,100
.44	40,400	35,700
.47	38,000	38,000
.50	35,300	40,600
.53	32,500	43,200
.56	29,800	45,800
.59	27,000	48,300

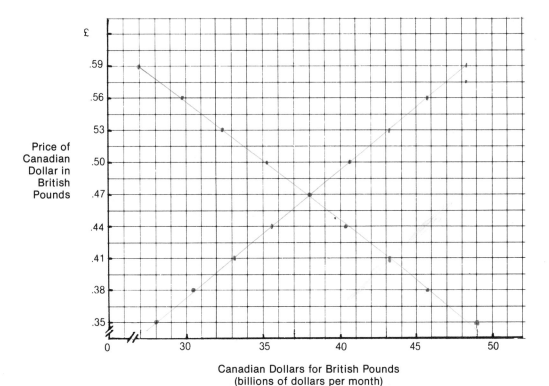

Canadian Dollars for British Pounds
(billions of dollars per month)

(a) What is the equilibrium rate of exchange in this market? _____.

Consider each of the following events taken separately and estimate what the resulting equilibrium exchange rate would be in each case, all other things being equal:

↑ supply

(b) The Canadian government buys the shares in Canadian-based petroleum companies that are held by residents of Britain, at a total cost of $3 billion. _____.

↑ demand

(c) British tourists spend $3 billion while visiting in Canada. _____.

↓ supply
~~demand~~

(d) The Canadian government decides to buy only Canadian-made defence goods and reduces its purchases of British military equipment by $4 billion. _____.

(e) Suppose the Canadian government decides to maintain the exchange rate of C$1.00 = £0.41. How would it do this and how many dollars would be involved each month? _____

_____

_____

_____

QUESTIONS FOR REVIEW AND DISCUSSION

1. Chapter 8 showed that there are several steps or links in the process by which a change in the money supply has its effect on employment, prices, and output. Is this the reason there is said to be a long lag in the effect of monetary policy?

2. Why is monetary policy likely to be more effective in curtailing inflation than in reducing unemployment?

3. What is the opportunity cost associated with accumulating foreign exchange reserves in the government's Foreign Exchange Account?

4. Who supplies the Canadian dollars in the foreign exchange markets?

5. Distinguish between an increase in the money supply in Canada and an increase in the supply of Canadian dollars on the foreign exchange markets.

6. During the period from July to November, 1981, there was much debate about whether Canada should maintain its high-interest-rate policy.

    (a) Some economists were quoted (*The Globe and Mail*, Toronto, 18 November 1981) who estimated that a decline of 4 percentage points in the interest rates in Canada (from a prime rate of 18 per cent), with no change in American interest rates, would reduce the value of the Canadian dollar by three cents (to about US$0.81), and by as much as six cents if the interest rate differential continued for a year or more. Explain why this decline in the dollar's values would occur.

    (b) A drop in the value of the Canadian dollar by this amount would be expected to increase inflation by about 15 per cent, or from 11.9 per cent to 13.7 per cent. Why would this likely occur?

    (c) The president of the Canadian Chamber of Commerce said that "it wouldn't hurt the country a bit if the dollar fell a few cents". Why might he say this?

7. The Governor of the Bank of Canada has been quoted as saying that the Bank has no targets for the foreign exchange rate of the Canadian dollar, though it does pay attention to it. "After all, it's the most important price in the Canadian economy" (*Financial Post*, 2 February 1988). What does the Governor mean when he says that the foreign exchange rate is the most important price in the Canadian economy?

Appendix:

8. Discuss the advantages and disadvantages of using the following as the means for international payments: (a) gold, (b) major foreign currencies, (c) SDRs.

9. In what respects is a "managed float" like a pegged exchange rate, and in what respects is it like a floating exchange rate?

11   Monetary, Fiscal, or Other Policies?

IMPORTANT TERMS AND CONCEPTS

Be sure you can define or explain each of these terms before proceeding with the questions and problems.

Keynesians
monetary (Friedman) rule
monetarism

labour supply policy
prices and incomes policy
supply-side policies

MULTIPLE-CHOICE QUESTIONS

Circle the letter corresponding with the most appropriate answer for each question.

1. The monetarists argue that expansionary fiscal policy:

   (a) has its effect through the monetary expansion that accompanies it
   (b) is ineffective because governments usually make the wrong decisions
   (c) slows the growth of aggregate expenditure in high unemployment conditions
   (d) is also necessary if expansionary monetary policy is to be effective

2. Advocates of fiscal policy:

   (a) believe that the government makes better decisions than the Bank of Canada
   (b) argue that government spending should represent a larger share of the GDP
   (c) argue that the effects of monetary policy are slower and less predictable than the effects of fiscal policy
   (d) believe that only fiscal policy can overcome the problem of an outward-shifting short-run Phillips curve

3. One major reason it proves to be so difficult to manage an economy through monetary and fiscal policy is that:

   (a) the time lags involved in the operation of either policy are often variable and sometimes long
   (b) the multiplier is actually quite a bit lower than $1/(1 - MPC)$
   (c) the Bank of Canada cannot initiate with much certainty a contraction in the money supply
   (d) demand-pull inflation is unresponsive to monetary and fiscal policy

4. The Friedman rule for monetary policy is that:

   (a) interest rates should be held constant by the central bank
   (b) money supply changes should be designed to offset cyclical changes in the unemployment rate
   (c) money supply should be increased annually at the rate projected for real growth in GDP
   (d) monetary policy should reinforce fiscal policy

5. When governments introduce a prices and incomes policy (or wage and price controls), they apparently are assuming:

   (a) that there will be general support for the policy
   (b) that inflation is primarily of the demand-pull type
   (c) that inflation is caused primarily by increasing prices of imports
   (d) that inflation is primarily of the cost-push type

6. It has been claimed that an anti-inflationary monetary policy based on high interest rates may cause further inflation:

   (a) due to the liquidity trap
   (b) because the velocity of money increases
   (c) because interest costs are part of sellers' total costs
   (d) due to all of the above factors

7. Many monetarists would like to see the Bank of Canada:

   (a) become more independent from the federal government
   (b) become more closely associated with the fiscal policy of the federal government
   (c) focus only on the foreign exchange rate
   (d) focus only on the level of interest rates

TRUE/FALSE QUESTIONS

State whether each of the following statements is true or false, or whether you are uncertain because the statement may be either true or false depending on the relevant circumstances and/or assumptions. Explain the reasons for your answer in each case.

1. If monetary and fiscal policies were properly designed and implemented, they would be sufficient to deal with inflation and unemployment.

2. Rising interest rates lead to rising prices.

3. Monetarists argue that changes in the money supply have a direct effect, as well as indirect effects resulting from changes in the interest rate.

4. The objective of monetary policy based on "rules" or "targets" is to maintain the money supply at a constant level.

5. The debate between monetarists and Keynesians is solely a debate about applying positive economics.

6. Labour supply policies are intended to reduce both inflation and unemployment.

7. A prices and incomes policy is intended to reduce both inflation and unemployment.

QUESTIONS FOR REVIEW AND DISCUSSION

1. Distinguish between discretionary monetary policy and monetary targets. Does it mean that monetarism has failed if the targets are changed periodically?

2. "If economists could obtain more accurate, up-to-date data on the aggregate economic activity of the economy, fiscal and monetary policy could eliminate inflation and unemployment." Do you agree? Explain carefully.

3. How are incomes policies expected to have an effect on high rates of inflation? Why have incomes policies generally not been very successful in controlling inflation?

12 Economic Growth and Productivity

IMPORTANT TERMS AND CONCEPTS

Be sure you can define or explain each of these terms before proceeding with
the questions and problems.

economic growth

potential output

technological change and
  technological progress

total-factor productivity

labour productivity

real vs. nominal GDP

standard of living

quality of life

social capital infrastructure

rate of time preference

capital/labour ratio

entrepreneurship

length of production run

service sector

supply-side policies

industrial strategy

MULTIPLE-CHOICE QUESTIONS

Circle the letter corresponding with the most appropriate answer for each
question.

1. Labour productivity in Canada:

    (a) is the same as total-factor productivity
    (b) was lower in the 1980s than it was in the 1950s
    (c) increases in proportion to the size of the labour force
    (d) varies with the length of the work week

2. The measure of economic growth is an imperfect measure of the standard of living because it does not take into account:

    (a) a reduction in the work week
    (b) improved quality of goods and services
    (c) increased pollution and congestion
    (d) all of the above

3. Economic growth is expected to improve income distribution by:

   (a) a "trickle-down" of spending from the wealthy to the poor
   (b) an increased willingness to support governments' redistribution programs
   (c) reducing inflation
   (d) none of the above

4. "Social capital infrastructure" includes all of the following, *except*:

   (a) hospitals
   (b) high schools
   (c) highways
   (d) hotels

5. The costs or disadvantages associated with economic growth include:

   (a) postponement of current consumption
   (b) adverse effects on the environment
   (c) obsolescence of some labour skills
   (d) all of the above

6. The real GDP per capita in Canada increased during the period 1930 to 1990 at an average annual rate of about:

   (a) 2.5 per cent
   (b) 5.0 per cent
   (c) 12.5 per cent
   (d) none of the above

7. Canada's economic growth for the period 1950 to 1967 has been attributed mainly to:

   (a) an increase in the quantity of labour
   (b) an improvement in labour productivity
   (c) an increase in number of hours worked
   (d) none of the above

8. Canada's annual economic growth rates during the past 20 years:

   (a) have been higher than in Japan and Germany
   (b) have been about the same as in Japan and Germany
   (c) have been lower than in Japan and Germany
   (d) cannot be compared with those in Japan and Germany

9. An important factor in Canada's lower rate of economic growth has been:

   (a) an inadequate supply of raw materials
   (b) shorter production runs
   (c) a higher degree of risk-taking
   (d) inadequate technical skills

10. The declining labour productivity in Canada has been attributed to:

    (a) a declining capital/labour ratio
    (b) the relatively greater growth of the service sector
    (c) higher prices for petroleum and electricity
    (d) all of the above

11. An "industrial strategy" has not been adopted in Canada because:

    (a) the emphasis for growth has been on the service sector
    (b) it is difficult to decide which industries should be supported in such a strategy
    (c) there is a federal-provincial disagreement over the funding of such a policy
    (d) it would require too much financial assistance from government

TRUE/FALSE QUESTIONS

State whether each of the following statements is true or false, or whether you are uncertain because the statement may be either true or false depending on the relevant circumstances and/or assumptions. Explain the reasons for your answer in each case.

1. A sudden increase in the labour force can cause a decline in labour productivity.

2. Economic growth in Canada during the 1950s and 1960s was due mainly to the higher levels of foreign investment.

3. Labour productivity has increased gradually in Canada during the past two decades.

4. The increase in oil prices may have been a factor in decreasing productivity.

5. Real GDP is always less than nominal GDP.

6. The value estimated for total-factor productivity will always be greater than that for labour productivity.

7. A difference of one percentage point in an economy's growth rate will have very little effect on the level of real income over a decade or two.

8. Canada spends a lower percentage of its GDP on research and development than do most industrialized countries.

PROBLEMS

1. Given the following data for an economy for 1992:

nominal GDP	$300 billion
total labour income	$225 billion
GDP implicit price index	150 (1986 = 100)
population	20 million

   Calculate:
   (a) real GDP _____
   (b) real GDP per capita _____
   (c) labour productivity _____

2. Calculate, using the Rule of 72 (see text, p. 291, fn. 2), how many years it would take for the real per capita GDP to double if it increases at an annual rate of:
   6% _____; 3% _____; 1% _____.

3. Suppose that the population increases by 1 per cent per year, the labour force increases by 1.5 per cent, the hours worked by each labourer decrease by 0.5 per cent, labour productivity improves by 2.0 per cent, and all else is constant. Calculate the percentage increase in the real GDP per capita. _____

QUESTIONS FOR REVIEW AND DISCUSSION

1. Why is measurement of productivity considered to be only an indirect measure of economic growth? How are these two measures related?

2. Discuss the limitations on real GDP per capita as a measure of individual well-being in Canada.

3. Distinguish between the productivity of labour and the productivity of capital, and then show how these are closely related.

4. What factors offer the greatest potential for increases in productivity in Canada during the next decade? Why? What policies, if any, might the federal and provincial governments implement to encourage this growth?

5. Why might an increase in energy prices cause declining productivity?

6. "Industrial strategy" is a popular term, but what exactly is meant by strategy in this context, what industries would be involved, and how is this policy expected to improve economic growth?

13 International Trade and the Balance of Payments

IMPORTANT TERMS AND CONCEPTS

Be sure you can define or explain each of these terms before proceeding with the questions and problems.

Canada-United States
   Automotive Agreement
absolute advantage
comparative advantage
terms of trade
export duties
ad valorem tariff
specific tariff
quota
embargo
sanction
retaliation
"infant industry" argument
GATT
"most-favoured nation" clause
non-tariff barriers
free trade area
customs union
common market

foreign exchange rate
pegged exchange rate
floating exchange rate
balance of payments
   disequilibrium (surplus or deficit)
appreciation
depreciation
devaluation
revaluation
overvalued currency
undervalued currency
exchange controls
Balance of International
   Payments (or balance of
   payments)
balance of trade
current account
capital account
basic balance

MULTIPLE-CHOICE QUESTIONS

Circle the letter corresponding with the most appropriate answer for each question.

1. Canada's exports in recent years have been about what percentage of the GDP?

(a) 15
(b) 25
(c) 35
(d) 45

2. Canada's exports to the United States in recent years have represented about what percentage of Canada's total exports?

   (a) 25
   (b) 50
   (c) 75
   (d) 90

3. If Canada could produce every commodity with exactly half the resources required to produce each commodity in the United States:

   (a) there would be no trade between the two countries
   (b) Canada would export goods to the United States but would import nothing
   (c) Canada would specialize in the production of those goods in which it had a comparative advantage
   (d) trade would take place between the two countries with Canada's benefit being twice that realized by the United States

4. Under conditions of increasing opportunity costs for a country's major exported commodity:

   (a) countries will realize economies of scale by specializing
   (b) the limits of the terms of trade will increase
   (c) the benefits of specialization in accordance with comparative advantage will diminish
   (d) the benefits of specialization in accordance with comparative advantage will increase

5. The limits to the terms of trade are determined by:

   (a) The General Agreement on Tariffs and Trade
   (b) the opportunity cost of producing a given good in each country
   (c) the foreign exchange rate between the two countries
   (d) the supply and demand conditions in each country

6. An argument in favour of tariffs that is consistent with the principle of comparative advantage is the:

   (a) maintenance of full employment
   (b) increased government revenues
   (c) improved balance of payments
   (d) development of economies of scale in selected industries

7. The basic argument against tariffs is that they:

   (a) encourage retaliation by other countries
   (b) interfere with the development of foreign trade based on comparative advantage
   (c) raise only small amounts in tax revenues
   (d) are so difficult to administer

8. Canada's history of tariff policy has included all but which of the following?

   (a) reduction of tariffs under the National Policy in the 1880s
   (b) lower tariffs on British imports introduced in 1899
   (c) increased tariffs in 1930 in response to the Depression
   (d) reduction of tariffs in the late 1960s

9. The GATT "most-favoured nation" clause means:

   (a) that Canada imposes lower tariffs on British imports
   (b) that tariffs are lower on imports from NATO countries
   (c) that a tariff reduction for one country's imports must be extended to imports of the same good from other countries
   (d) preferential tariffs for the less developed countries

10. A customs union:

   (a) restricts trade with all countries by imposing tariffs
   (b) provides for free trade among countries within the union, and a common set of tariffs against countries outside the union
   (c) provides for free trade among countries within the union, and different tariffs set by each country against countries outside the union
   (d) permits free movement of goods, labour, and capital among countries within the nation

11. Under a system of flexible exchange rates, a deficit in Canada's trade with Japan (*ceteris paribus*) will cause:

   (a) an increase in the dollar price of yen
   (b) an increase in the yen price of the dollar
   (c) an increase in the money supply in Canada
   (d) a long-run disequilibrium in Canada's trade balance

12. An increase in the exchange rate of the Canadian dollar likely would result in:

   (a) a decrease in the rate of inflation
   (b) an increase in the unemployment rate
   (c) a decrease in the current account surplus (or increase in the deficit)
   (d) all of the above

13. The supply of Canadian dollars exchanged for German marks will increase if:

    (a) the price of the Canadian dollar remains constant in terms of marks
    (b) German banks make loans to a provincial government in Canada
    (c) Canada decides to increase the size and number of its defence forces in Germany
    (d) Canadians sharply reduce their purchase of German-made automobiles

14. The value of the Canadian dollar in terms of francs will tend to depreciate when:

    (a) Canadian tourists increase their expenditures while travelling in France
    (b) French investors establish a tire manufacturing plant in Quebec
    (c) French tourists increase their expenditures while travelling in Canada
    (d) a French bank makes a major loan to the provincial government in Quebec

15. If there is a surplus in the combined current and capital accounts of Canada's balance of payments, this means that:

    (a) there is an increase in Canada's holdings of foreign exchange and gold
    (b) there is a decrease in Canada's holdings of foreign exchange and gold
    (c) there must be a surplus on current account
    (d) there must be a surplus on capital account

16. Which of the following does *not* involve payments of Canadian dollars to other countries?

    (a) immigrants sending money to parents "back home"
    (b) Canadian tourists' spending in Europe
    (c) sale of a Canadian corporation's bonds to an American firm
    (d) imports of foreign automobiles

17. When a Canadian firm sells nickel to a British firm, this:

    (a) appears as a credit entry in Canada's balance of trade
    (b) appears as a credit entry in Britain's balance of trade
    (c) appears as a debit entry in Canada's balance of trade
    (d) does not affect Canada's balance of trade because there is an offsetting entry in the capital account

18. In the revised Balance of Payments accounts, Canadian residents' receipts of interest and dividends from abroad appear in the:

   (a) transfers account
   (b) services account
   (c) short-term capital account
   (d) investment income account

TRUE/FALSE QUESTIONS

State whether each of the following statements is true or false, or whether you are uncertain because the statement may be either true or false depending on the relevant circumstances and/or assumptions. Explain the reasons for your answer in each case.

1. For a country on a fixed foreign exchange rate, devaluation of its currency will not necessarily reduce its balance of payments deficit.

2. Even if there is a deficit on both the current account and the capital account, the balance of payments will still be balanced.

3. The principle of comparative advantage can be applied to trade between regions within a country as well as between countries.

4. A tariff is beneficial to the country that imposes the tariff but harmful to the country whose exports are subject to the tariff.

5. One valid economic argument for tariffs is that they increase the government's revenues.

6. A decrease in the foreign exchange value of the Canadian dollar would likely lead to a reduction in unemployment in Canada.

7. Pegging or fixing the foreign exchange rate at an official level removes the threat of speculation against the value of that currency.

8. The only situation in which international trade is not advantageous to a country is when the country has an absolute advantage in the production of all commodities and is at full employment.

PROBLEMS

1. Suppose that two countries, Agro and Indus, can produce only two commodities, wheat and apples. Assume that labour is the only input and that one unit of labour will yield the following quantities of *either* commodity:

	Wheat (kilograms)	Apples (kilograms)
Agro	6	2
Indus	4	1

(a) The opportunity cost of one kilogram of wheat in Agro is _____; in Indus it is _____. The opportunity cost of one kilogram of apples in Agro is _____; in Indus it is _____.

(b) Agro has an absolute advantage in _____ and a comparative advantage in _____; Indus has an absolute advantage in _____ and a comparative advantage in _____.

(c) If international trade is to be beneficial to both countries, the terms of trade must be between what ratios? _____ and _____. Agro would export _____ and Indus would export _____.

(d) If there is a technological improvement in Agro such that it can produce 8 kilograms of wheat with one unit of labour, would this have any effect on trade between Agro and Indus? _____.

Explain: _____

_____

_____

_____

(e) On the graph below, and using the data from the above table, draw the consumption possibility curves *before* and *after* trade for Agro and Indus, assuming trade occurs at a ratio of 3.5W:1A and that each country produces the commodity in which it has a comparative advantage and trades this with the other country. Assume also that each country has 60 units of labour available. Label the curves *A* and *I* for Agro and Indus, and *BT* and *AT* for before trade and after trade.

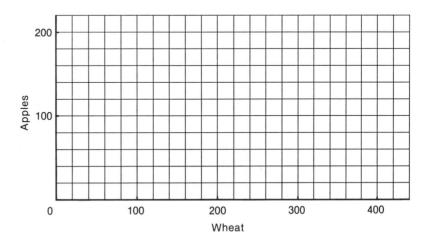

2. Suppose the exchange rate is US$.90 = C$1.00, and assume further that each week Canada sells 1,000 units of export goods at a price of C$1.00, while importing 1,000 units of American goods priced at US$.90. There are no transportation costs or import duties.

If over the range of prices involved in this question the elasticity of demand for Canada's exports is 0.7 and its elasticity of demand for imports is 0.5, and the exchange rate is then pegged at par (US$1.00 = C$1.00), one could expect that:

(a) Canada will now export _____ units per week to the United States, priced at C$ _____, for total export receipts of C$ _____.

Explain, showing your calculations here, how you estimated these answers:

_____

_____

_____

_____

(b) Canada will now import _____ units per week from the United States, at a price per unit of C$ _____, for a total expenditure of C$ _____.

Explain, showing your calculations here, how you estimated these answers:

_____

_____

_____

_____

_____

(c) The balance of trade in Canada previously showed a (balance/ deficit/surplus) and after the revaluation of the Canadian dollar, the balance of trade shows a (balance/deficit/surplus).

3. Suppose that the Canadian demand for Swiss-made watches is as shown in the table below:

Exchange Rate (Canadian Dollars for Swiss Francs)	Price of Watch in Switzerland (francs)	Price of Watch in Canadian Dollars	Quantity of Watches Demanded (per month)	Total Canadian Dollars Supplied	Total Swiss Francs Demanded
C$1 = SF2	144	72	500	36 00	72 000
C$1 = SF3	144	48	800	38 400	115 200
C$1 = SF4	144	36	1200	43 200	172 800

(a) Calculate the Canadian dollar price of Swiss watches at each exchange rate and the total Canadian dollars that would be supplied in exchange for Swiss francs to purchase the desired number of watches. Assume there are no tariffs and no transportation costs. Plot the supply of Canadian dollars on the graph provided.

Price of
Canadian
Dollars in
Swiss Francs

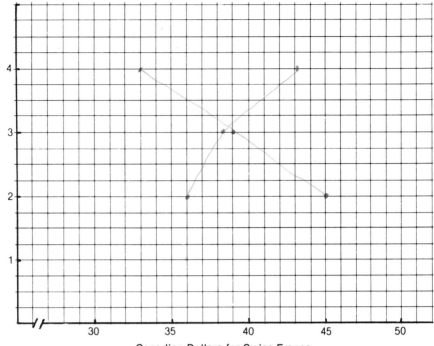

Canadian Dollars for Swiss Francs
(thousands of dollars per month)

(b) Suppose that the Swiss demand for Canadian-made whisky is as
shown in the table below. (For simplicity assume there are no taxes
on whisky in either country.) Calculate the Swiss franc prices of
whisky and the total Canadian dollars that would be demanded in
exchange for Swiss francs to purchase the desired quantity of
whisky at each exchange rate.

Plot the demand for Canadian dollars on the same graph.

Exchange Rate	Price of Whisky in Canada (per litre)	Price of Whisky in Swiss Francs	Quantity of Whisky Demanded (per month)	Total Canadian Dollars Demanded	Total Swiss Francs Supplied
SF1 = C$.50	$3.00	6	15,000	45 000	90,000
SF1 = C$.33	3.00	9	13,000	39,000	117,000
SF1 = C$.25	3.00	12	11,000	33,000	132,000

(c) The Canadian demand for Swiss watches in terms of Canadian dollars is (elastic/unitary/inelastic) and the Swiss demand for Canadian whisky in terms of Swiss francs is (elastic/unitary/inelastic).

(d) The trade in watches and whisky is the only trade between Canada and Switzerland. In this case, the equilibrium price of the Canadian dollar in Swiss francs is _____.

(e) If the countries were on a pegged exchange rate of C$1 = SF2, what would be the consequences? _____

_____

_____

Should Canada put an export tax on whisky? _____. Should Switzerland put a tariff on whisky? _____. Explain. _____

_____

_____

4. Indicate with an X in the proper column where payments for each of the following items would appear in Canada's Balance of International Payments:

	Current Account				
	Goods	Services	Invest-ment Income	Trans-fers	Capital Account
(a) sale of common shares in a Canadian firm to British buyers	_____	_____	_____	_____	_____
(b) Canadian purchases of French bicycles	_____	_____	_____	_____	_____
(c) interest paid on Ontario government bonds to Swiss bank	_____	_____	_____	_____	_____
(d) dividends received by Canadians from United States	_____	_____	_____	_____	_____
(e) repayment of an Ontario Hydro loan from New York	_____	_____	_____	_____	_____
(f) American tourist ticket purchases from Air Canada	_____	_____	_____	_____	_____
(g) Canada Wheat Board sale of wheat to the Soviet Union	_____	_____	_____	_____	_____
(h) Canadian government foreign aid contribution to India	_____	_____	_____	_____	_____

5. Given the following data for an economy's Balance of International Payments:

	Payments	Receipts
Merchandise	25,000	24,000
Services	4,000	5,000
Investment income	1,000	1,000
Transfers	1,000	500
Direct investment	500,000	450,000
Portfolio investment	800,000	850,000
Bank deposits	1,000,000	1,200,000
Short-term credit	4,000,000	395,000

Calculate the following:

(a) Balance of trade   _____

(b) Current account balance   _____

(c) Long-term capital account balance   _____

(d) Short-term capital account balance   _____

QUESTIONS FOR REVIEW AND DISCUSSION

1. Why is comparative advantage, rather than absolute advantage, the relevant concept for explaining international trade?

2. "International trade is indirect production." Explain.

3. "A tariff cannot be effective in providing government revenues if it provides effective protection for domestic producers." Do you agree? Explain.

4. Discuss the relative advantages and disadvantages of import tariffs and quotas as a method for protecting domestic industries in the short run.

5. Why do policy-makers seem to be more concerned with the balance of trade or the balance on current account than with the balance on capital account?

6. A deficit in the balance of trade indicates that a country is enjoying a higher standard of living than if there were no deficit. Why then do governments try to reduce trade deficits?

7. What are the possible effects of a decline in the Canadian dollar exchange rate on (a) the balance of payments, (b) the level of employment, and (c) the rate of inflation? Explain how these effects would occur.

8. Should Canada have a fixed or floating foreign exchange rate? Give a detailed explanation for your position.

14   Economics of the Public Sector

IMPORTANT TERMS AND CONCEPTS

Be sure you can define or explain each of these terms before proceeding with the questions and problems.

public sector
transfer payments
government functions
benefit-cost analysis
PPBS
principles of taxation
equity
neutrality
efficiency
benefits-received principle
ability-to-pay principle
equal treatment of equals
regressive tax

proportional tax
progressive tax
direct taxes
indirect taxes
marginal tax rate
capital gain
tax brackets
excise tax
tax credits
tax abatements
equalization payments

MULTIPLE-CHOICE QUESTIONS

Circle the letter corresponding with the most appropriate answer for each question.

1. Total expenditures by all levels of government combined, including transfer payments, are currently about what percentage of the Canadian GDP?

   (a) 15
   (b) 25
   (c) 45
   (d) 65

2. The percentage of total government spending allocated to health, education and social welfare in Canada is approximately:

   (a) 10 per cent
   (b) 25 per cent
   (c) 50 per cent
   (d) 75 per cent

3. The federal government's total expenditures in recent years have been:

   (a) greater than the combined expenditures of the provincial and municipal governments
   (b) greater than the provincial governments' expenditures but less than the total for municipal governments
   (c) greater than the municipal governments' expenditures but less than the total for provincial governments
   (d) greater than the total expenditures of either the provincial governments or the municipal governments

4. Benefit-cost analysis is a technique for determining:

   (a) which commodities can be classified as public goods
   (b) which commodities should be produced in the private sector
   (c) whether a particular government program represents a reasonable allocation of resources
   (d) whether a particular tax is equitable

5. The benefits-received principle of taxation is difficult to apply equitably in some cases because:

   (a) benefits of some government services "spill over" to the persons other than the ones who receive or use the services directly
   (b) some government programs provide no benefits
   (c) people do not benefit equally from government services
   (d) no one would use the services if the government charged for them directly

6. Which of the following statements does *not* correctly describe the ability-to-pay principle of taxation?

   (a) it has general appeal on equity grounds, but there are problems in applying the principle in specific cases
   (b) it is difficult to reach agreement on how differently to treat people with differing ability to pay
   (c) equal values in property holdings do not necessarily indicate equal ability to pay
   (d) taxes based on the ability-to-pay principle will be regressive

7. The ability-to-pay principle of taxation is most evident in:

   (a) gasoline tax
   (b) property tax
   (c) progressive income tax
   (d) general sales tax

8. If one pays a tax of $200 on $1,000 income, $300 tax on $2,000 income, and $400 tax on $3,000 income, the tax is described as:

   (a) progressive
   (b) proportional
   (c) regressive
   (d) equitable

9. The major source of tax revenue for the federal government is:

   (a) property taxes
   (b) sales and excise taxes
   (c) corporate income taxes
   (d) personal income taxes

10. The major source of tax revenues for municipalities is:

   (a) property taxes
   (b) sales and excise taxes
   (c) corporate income taxes
   (d) personal income taxes

TRUE/FALSE QUESTIONS

State whether each of the following statements is true or false, or whether you are uncertain because the statement may be either true or false depending on the relevant circumstances and/or assumptions. Explain the reasons for your answer in each case.

1. The growth of government expenditures has been due mainly to increased expenditure for education, health, and welfare.

2. Economists generally agree that the only role for government intervention in an economy is to stabilize the level of economic activity.

3. Benefit-cost analysis is intended to assist governments in determining how funds should be allocated between various programs.

4. Economic considerations would suggest that the federal government is the most appropriate level of government to provide most public services.

5. The "spillover benefits" argument leads to the conclusion that education should be provided and financed by local governments.

6. In determining who should pay any given tax, it is easier to decide who benefits by a service than who is best able to pay for the service.

7. The only fair tax system is a proportional income tax.

8. Sales taxes are indirect taxes.

9. Under a progressive income tax, the marginal tax rate does not change.

PROBLEMS

1. Suppose that personal incomes are taxed according to the following simplified and hypothetical schedule:

Income	Tax Paid	Marginal Income	Marginal Tax Paid	Marginal Tax Rate (%)	Average Tax Rate (%)	After-Tax Income
$ 0	$ 0				0	0
		2000	200	10		
2,000	200				10	1800
		3000	450	15		
5,000	650				13	
		3000	750	(25)		
8,000	1,400				17.5	6600
		4000	1200	30		
12,000	2,600				21.7	
		8000	2800	35		
20,000	5.400				27	
		20,000	8000	40		
40,000	13,400				33.5	26,600

(a) Complete the above schedules by calculating the marginal tax rates between different income levels, and then the average tax rates and after-tax income. (In this simple tax system there are no personal exemptions.)

(b) This tax structure is (regressive/proportional/progressive).

(c) If a person who currently earns $5,000 before tax wishes to increase his after-tax income by $1,000, how much additional income must this person earn? _____   *mag tax = 2 5 %* $\frac{1000}{.75}$

(d) The person who earns $40,000 has a before-tax income that is five times that of a person with a $8,000 income, but in after-tax terms, the higher income is _____ times greater than the lower income.

(e) Although the $12,000 income-earner will be at a marginal tax rate of __35__ per cent on the next $2,000 earned, the total taxes paid will be only _____ per cent of the $14,000 total income.
23.6

2. The figure below shows the relationship of taxes and income for different types of taxes:

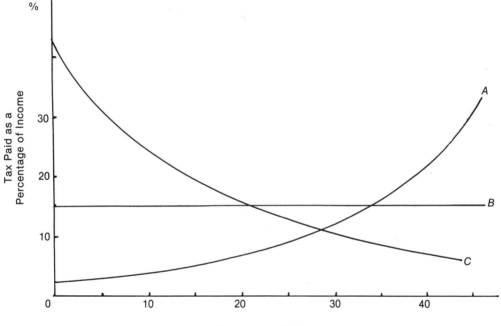

Income (thousands of dollars per year)

(a) A regressive tax is represented by curve _____.
    A progressive tax is represented by curve _____.
    A proportional tax is represented by curve _____.

(b) The income tax system in question 1 is better represented by curve _____ than by either of the other two curves.

(c) The curve that represents a progessive tax shows that this particular tax becomes (more/less) progressive as income increases; and the regressive tax becomes (more/less) regressive.

QUESTIONS FOR REVIEW AND DISCUSSION

1. Why has the total government share of GDP increased so much over the past decade? What should this percentage be? Why?

2. Should governments provide any services they do not now provide? Are there any services currently provided by governments that should be provided instead by the private sector? Specify and explain why in terms of the principles outlined in this chapter.

3. Do you favour the ability-to-pay or the benefits-received principle of taxation? Why? Which principle is the easier one to apply? Which of the taxes collected by any level of government do you favour and which do you oppose most strongly? Why?

4. Do you think a tax on gasoline is progressive, proportional, or regressive? Why?

5. To which government programs might benefit-cost analysis be applied most easily? For which programs would it be difficult to do benefit-cost analysis? What are the key characteristics that determine how easy or difficult it is to apply benefit-cost analysis to different programs?

6. An automobile mechanic was overheard saying, "The government should stay right out of the whole business of designing automobiles. People know best what they want." Do you agree? Explain.

PART THREE

Consumers and Producers

15 Consumer Demand

IMPORTANT TERMS AND CONCEPTS

Be sure you can define or explain each of these terms before proceeding with the questions and problems.

utility
marginal utility
total utility
law of diminishing marginal utility
utility maximization rule
price vs. value
consumer surplus
substitution effect
income effect
Engel's Law

Appendix:

indifference schedule
indifference curve
indifference map
marginal rate of substitution
diminishing marginal rate of
  substitution
budget line
consumer equilibrium

MULTIPLE-CHOICE QUESTIONS

Circle the letter corresponding with the most appropriate answer for each question.

1. Marginal utility:

   (a) increases as one consumes more of a good
   (b) decreases as one consumes more of a good
   (c) is always negative
   (d) is always constant

2. A consumer obtains the greatest possible total satisfaction or utility with the income available if the consumer:

   (a) purchases the goods yielding the highest utility, regardless of price
   (b) purchases goods that have the lowest prices
   (c) purchases quantitites of various goods such that the marginal utility of each is equal to the total utility realized from each
   (d) purchases quantities of various goods such that the marginal utility per dollar spent for each good is the same for each good

3. Suppose that MUx/Px is greater than MUy/Py. To increase total utility, the consumer should:

   (a) buy more of Y and less of X
   (b) buy more of Y only if its price falls
   (c) buy less of X only if its price rises
   (d) buy more of X and less of Y

4. If the price of a product could be varied according to consumers' marginal utility for the product, consumer surplus:

   (a) would not exist
   (b) would decrease with increasing quantity purchased
   (c) would remain constant
   (d) would increase with increasing quantity purchased

5. Consumer surplus is the difference between:

   (a) a consumer's income and total expenditures
   (b) total utility and marginal utility at any given level of consumption
   (c) the quantity demanded and the quantity supplied at a given price
   (d) the actual expenditure for a given quantity of a good and the total amount that consumers would be willing to pay

6. Engel's Law states that:

   (a) as the price of a commodity declines, a greater quantity will be purchased
   (b) as a consumer's income increases, a lower percentage is spent for food
   (c) as a consumer's income increases, a larger percentage is spent for food
   (d) as consumption of a commodity increases, the marginal utility declines

Appendix:

7. As a consumer moves downward along an indifference curve, the total satisfaction realized by the consumer:

   (a) increases
   (b) decreases
   (c) remains constant
   (d) increases at a decreasing rate

8. A positive "income effect" indicates that:

   (a) when the price of a product falls, a consumer will be able to buy more of it with a given money income
   (b) consumers vary the quantities of various goods purchased until the marginal utility from the last unit of each good purchased is the same
   (c) when the price of a product falls, the lower price will induce the consumer to buy more of that product and less of other products
   (d) an increase in money income will cause consumers to buy lower quantities of normal goods

9. The "substitution effect" indicates that:

   (a) when the price of a product falls, a consumer will be able to buy more of it with a given money income
   (b) consumers vary the quantities of various goods purchased until the marginal utility from the last unit of each good purchased is the same
   (c) when the price of a product falls, the lower price will induce the consumer to buy more of that product and less of other products
   (d) an increase in money income will cause consumers to buy lower quantities of normal goods.

10. Which of the following statements is *incorrect*?

   (a) in an indifference map, the curve farthest to the upper right represents the highest level of satisfaction
   (b) the income and substitution effects of a price decrease normally work in the same direction (in terms of quantities purchased)
   (c) an increase in the price of a good with nothing else changed will likely force the consumer to a lower indifference curve
   (d) an indifference curve shows the different amounts of satisfaction derived from different quantities of a good

11. If a consumer's tastes change such that each combination of goods provides twice as much satisfaction as before (with no change in income or prices), the consumer will:

   (a) purchase more of each good, but the relative quantities will change
   (b) purchase twice as much of each good
   (c) purchase exactly half as much of each good as before
   (d) make no change in her purchases

TRUE/FALSE QUESTIONS

State whether each of the following statements is true or false, or whether you are uncertain because the statement may be either true or false depending on the relevant circumstances and/or assumptions. Explain the reasons for your answer in each case.

1. Assume that a consumer buys only X and Y. When the price of X falls, the consumer buys more X and less Y. It can therefore be concluded that X is a normal good and Y is an inferior good.

2. Engel's Law implies that consumers have a high income-elasticity of demand for food.

3. Since we cannot measure utility directly, the whole concept of consumers' utility or satisfaction has become irrelevant to economic theory.

4. The lower the price charged for any given commodity, the greater will be the consumer surplus.

Appendix:

5. Indifference curves can never intersect.

6. The convex shape of indifference curves is due to the diminishing marginal rate of substitution.

7. The budget line is a straight line because a consumer's income does not vary with different combinations of the commodities.

8. A consumer can reach a higher level of satisfaction only by an increase in income, and not by a change in prices.

9. Suppose that two sisters, Maria and Ester, have very different indifference curves showing their relative preferences for books and for clothes. With books on the vertical axis, Maria's indifference curves have a very steep slope, while Ester's indifference curves have much less slope. We can therefore conclude that Maria is very fashion-conscious and only mildly interested in reading; Ester has less interest in clothes and more readily spends her income on books.

PROBLEMS

by trial error

1. Given the following information about a consumer's utility associated with goods X and Y:

Quantity	1	2	3	4	5	6	7
MUx	28	24	16	12	10	8	6
MUy	16	14	12	10	6	5	4

Money income is $26; price of X is $4; price of Y is $2.

(a) The consumer will maximize his or her utility by purchasing _____ units of X and _____ units of Y.

(b) If the consumer's money income was increased to $38, utility would be maximized by purchasing _____ units of X and _____ units of Y. If income remains at $38 but the price of X increases to $6, the consumer would maximize utility by purchasing _____ units of X and _____ units of Y.

(c) What is the total utility associated with the consumption of 5 units of commodity X? _____. Can total utility be positive if, for example, the marginal utility associated with the 10th unit of X is negative? _____. Can total utility be increasing when marginal utility is positive but decreasing? _____.

Appendix:

2. Assume the following information concerning an individual's satisfaction associated with the consumption of ice cream cones and chocolate bars each month. Round your answers to complete units.

Combinations yielding equal levels of satisfaction:

Level One		Level Two		Level Three		Level Four	
Bars	**Cones**	**Bars**	**Cones**	**Bars**	**Cones**	**Bars**	**Cones**
15	1	12	4	12	7	13	10
11	2	10	5	10	8	10	12
9	3	7	7	7	11	9	13
4	8	5	11	5	15	6	18
3	10	4	14	4	20	5	23

(a) Plot this information in Figure 15.1 and join the points given for each level in a smooth continuous curve to form four indifference curves. Label each curve.

Figure 15.1

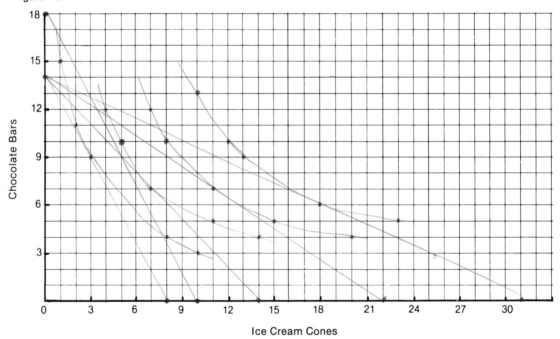

Ice Cream Cones

(b) Assume that the price of chocolate bars is $.60, the price of ice cream cones is $1.05, and that the individual's income available for expenditure on these two goods is $8.40 per month. Plot this person's budget line or income line on the graph. The combination that represents the highest level of satisfaction this person can reach with an income of $8.40 is (approximately) _____ chocolate bars and _____ ice cream cones. Why is it necessary to say "approximately" in this case? _____

_____

(c) Next, suppose that the price of ice cream cones falls, but that the individual's income and the price of chocolate bars are unchanged. Plot the new budget lines that are associated with each of the prices shown below and estimate the number of ice cream cones that would be purchased each month, at each of the alternative prices.

Demand for Cones

Price: $1.05 $.60 $.39 $.27

Quantity: ____   ____   ____   ____

(d) Calculate the elasticity between each price level.

(e) Plot the price and quantity data from part (c) above in Figure 15.2 and join the points with a smooth continuous curve to produce the individual's demand curve for ice cream. (Note that this demand curve is based on the assumptions specified in Chapter 3: the relative price of chocolate bars; the income available; and tastes or preferences — as expressed by the shape of the indifference curves.)

Figure 15.2

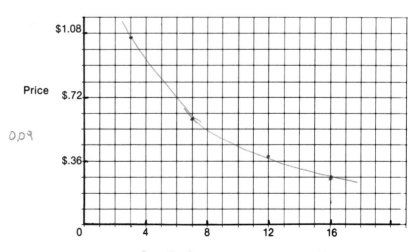

Quantity (ice cream cones per month)

(f) Now return to Figure 15.1, which shows four indifference curves. Suppose the prices of cones and bars remain as originally assumed, but that the individual's income increases from $8.40 to $10.80. Draw the new budget line and label it. Since this new budget line is tangent to the same indifference curve that was reached in part (c) when the price of cones fell to $.60, it is possible to calculate the "income effect" of this fall in the price of cones. The "income effect" is _____ cones and the "substitution effect" is _____ cones, for a total effect of _____ more cones purchased as the price fell from $1.05 to $.60.

3. In the diagrams below, draw budget lines that represent the specified conditions:

   (a) there is a 25 per cent decrease in the price of Y and a 50 per cent increase in the price of X, but no change in income.

   (b) the price of Y decreases and the price of X increases, such that there is no change in the consumer's maximum possible satisfaction

   (c) the prices of X and Y are unchanged, but the consumer's income increases by 25 per cent

   (d) the price of X rises by 50 per cent, income increases by 50 per cent, and the price of Y rises by 50 per cent.

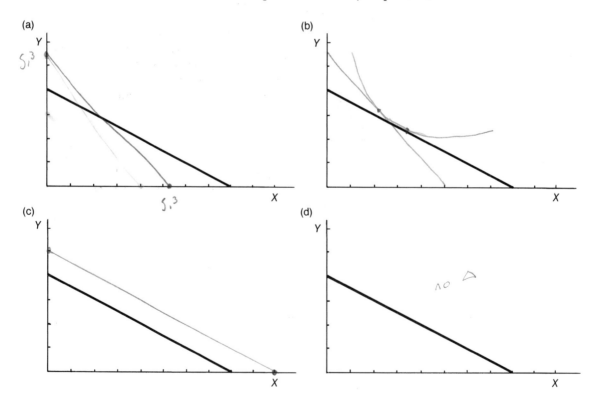

QUESTIONS FOR REVIEW AND DISCUSSION

1. "Consumer sovereignty is a fiction. Producers develop new products and then use advertising to persuade consumers that they should buy these products." Do you aree? Why?

2. Why does the optimum allocation of a consumer's income require the same ratio of marginal utility to price for all commodities purchased? What basic objective is assumed in stating this rule?

3. Since diminishing marginal utility seems to be encountered by all consumers, a government program that taxes the rich and gives the proceeds to the poor can be rationalized by this fact alone. Do you agree? Why?

4. Name three or four commodities for which you enjoy a substantial consumer surplus. Explain carefully why consumer surplus exists.

5. Suppose someone who has an average income says, "I really do need a new suit but I can't afford it." How would you explain this statement in terms of the theory of consumer behaviour?

6. "If a consumer's income elasticity of demand for some goods is greater than unity, there must be some goods for which the income elasticity is less than unity." Explain why you do or do not agree.

7. Assume that your tastes and relative prices remain unchanged but that you suddenly become five times better off financially than you are now. What would you expect to buy more of, less of, and in the same amount? What would you conclude about the income-elasticities of the commodities in each of these three categories? Is there any commodity for which the income-elasticity is zero?

Appendix:

8. Draw the indifference curves for the commodities in the following cases and explain your answer:

   (a) two commodities—skis and ski bindings—purchased separately; and
   (b) white eggs and brown eggs.

9. Explain in non-mathematical terms how the diminishing marginal rate of substitution is logically related to diminishing marginal utility.

16   Production Costs

IMPORTANT TERMS AND CONCEPTS

Be sure you can define or explain each of these terms before proceeding with the questions and problems.

opportunity cost
explicit cost
implicit cost
imputed cost
normal profit
economic or pure profit
short run
long run
production function
production schedule
total product
average product

marginal product
diminishing productivity
law of diminishing returns
law of variable proportions
fixed costs
variable costs
total cost
average cost (variable, total)
marginal cost
long-run average total cost
return to scale

MULTIPLE-CHOICE QUESTIONS

Circle the letter corresponding with the most appropriate answer for each question.

1. Pure profit is not a cost item because:
   (a) it cannot be calculated precisely
   (b) it need not be realized in order that a firm continue to produce the commodity concerned
   (c) it is retained by the firm
   (d) it is really part of the wage costs as a return to the owner's labour

2. A firm spends $100,000 for new equipment. The interest that would have been received had the firm purchased a $100,000 bond is termed:
   (a) explicit cost
   (b) implicit cost
   (c) long-run cost
   (d) short-run cost

3. When the marginal product is decreasing but is greater than the average product, the average product is:

   (a) increasing at an increasing rate
   (b) decreasing
   (c) increasing
   (d) at a maximum

4. The short run refers to the period of time:

   (a) too short for quantities of any inputs to be varied
   (b) long enough for quantities of all inputs to be varied
   (c) in which quantities of only some inputs can be varied
   (d) in which quantity of output cannot be varied

5. Which of the following is most likely to be a fixed cost?

   (a) expenditures for raw materials
   (b) real estate taxes
   (c) wages for unskilled labour
   (d) shipping charges

6. Which of the following is most likely to be a variable cost?

   (a) real estate taxes
   (b) property insurance premiums
   (c) leasing charges for special equipment
   (d) shipping charges

7. As the quantity of output is increased, under typical conditions:

   (a) the total cost rises and then falls
   (b) the average cost falls and then rises
   (c) the marginal cost declines
   (d) the average cost rises and then falls

8. The average product is equal to the marginal product:

   (a) when the marginal product is at a minimum
   (b) when the average product is at a maximum
   (c) when the total product is at a maximum
   (d) when the average product is increasing

9. Economies of scale are illustrated by:

   (a) the U-shape of the short-run average cost curve
   (b) the downward-sloping portion of the long-run cost curve
   (c) the downward-sloping portion of the marginal cost curve
   (d) the rising portion of the total cost curve

TRUE/FALSE QUESTIONS

State whether each of the following statements is true or false, or whether you are uncertain because the statement may be either true or false depending on the relevant circumstances and/or assumptions. Explain the reasons for your answer in each case.

1. The short-run average total cost curve is usually U-shaped.

2. The short-run average total cost curve can never be a straight line.

3. If marginal cost is rising, average cost may be either rising or falling.

4. Normal profit is included in the total cost when determining a firm's equilibrium output.

5. The short-run period could be the same as the long-run period.

6. The law of diminishing returns would not apply if all factors were completely variable.

7. The average fixed cost cannot increase with increasing levels of output.

8. Economies of scale usually occur with increasing levels of the variable factor.

PROBLEM

1. In the spaces provided below, draw the approximate shape of the marginal cost curve associated with the marginal product curve derived from each of the total product curves shown:

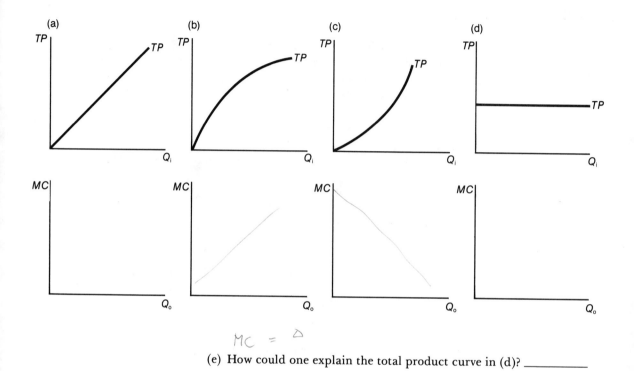

$$MC = \triangle$$

(e) How could one explain the total product curve in (d)? _____

_____

_____

_____

_____

QUESTIONS FOR REVIEW AND DISCUSSION

1. Why are normal profits, but not pure or economic profits, considered to be a cost of production?

2. Explain the relationship between marginal cost per unit of output and the law of diminishing marginal productivity.

3. Explain why the *MC* curve always intersects the *ATC* and *AVC* curves at the lowest points on these curves. Why does the *ATC* curve usually fall at low levels of output and then rise as output is increased further?

4. "The existence of economies of large scale contradicts the law of diminishing returns." Do you agree? Why? Which concept is relevant in the short run? Which is relevant in the long run? Explain.

17 Supply Decisions in Competitive Markets

IMPORTANT TERMS AND CONCEPTS

Be sure you can define or explain each of these terms before proceeding with the questions and problems.

market structure
perfect competition
price-takers
freedom of entry
momentary (or market) period
profit maximization
total revenue
marginal revenue
average revenue
shutdown price

short-run supply curve
firm
industry
industry supply curve
short-run equilibrium
long-run equilibrium
long-run supply curve
constant-cost industry
decreasing-cost industry
increasing-cost industry

MULTIPLE-CHOICE QUESTIONS

Circle the letter corresponding with the most appropriate answer for each question.

1. Which statement is *incorrect?*

   (a) the marginal cost curve intersects the average variable cost curve at its minimum point
   (b) a firm has a fixed cost of $50,000 and an output of 5,000 shirts per month. If the output drops to 2,500 shirts per month, fixed cost in the short run remains at $50,000
   (c) fixed costs remain constant in the long run
   (d) if a firm is producing a quantity of output such that its marginal revenue is greater than its original cost, it should increase its output to maximize profit

2. "Perfect competition" describes a market in which:

   (a) there are numerous suppliers
   (b) all firms produce identical products
   (c) each firm has access to all of the resources required
   (d) all of the above are true

3. Under perfect competition, the firm and the industry:

   (a) face infinitely elastic demand curves
   (b) face downward-sloping demand curves
   (c) face different demand curves; the firm faces a downward-sloping curve and the industry faces an infinitely elastic curve
   (d) face different demand curves; the firm faces an infinitely elastic curve and the industry faces a downward-sloping curve

4. The competitive firm's short-run supply curve is the segment of the marginal cost curve:

   (a) below the demand curve
   (b) above the average total cost curve
   (c) above the average variable cost curve
   (d) above the average fixed cost curve

5. An individual firm in a perfectly competitive market is described as a "price-taker" because:

   (a) there are no good substitutes for its product
   (b) prices depend only on consumers' demand
   (c) keen advertising by its competitors forces each firm to charge the same price
   (d) each firm supplies a minute fraction of the total supply to the market

6. Which of the following statements is *incorrect?*

   (a) in the momentary or market period, the quantity supplied is fixed
   (b) under pure competition, in the long run, each firm produces at the lowest possible average total cost
   (c) in order to construct the long-run supply curves of an industry, one must assume that the prices of all factors of production remain constant
   (d) none of a firm's short-run *ATC* curves ever lie below the firm's *LRATC*

TRUE/FALSE QUESTIONS

State whether each of the following statements is true or false, or whether you are uncertain because the statement may be either true or false depending on the relevant circumstances and/or assumptions. Explain the reasons for your answer in each case.

1. A competitive firm's short-run supply curve is usually upward-sloping to the right.

2. Firms are interested in maximizing their profits; but not in minimizing their losses.

3. If the government were to remove the sales tax on building materials, this would lower the price of housing.

4. An entrepreneur will always want to produce an output that will keep average total cost at a minimum, since this is the most efficient level of production.

5. A firm in perfect competition would produce only if it were making a profit.

6. Perfectly competitive firms operate with excess capacity in the long run.

7. For a perfectly competitive firm, marginal revenue is constant and is equal to the average revenue, or price.

PROBLEMS

1. Below is the set of short-run costs curves for a firm in a perfectly competitive industry:

Figure 17.1

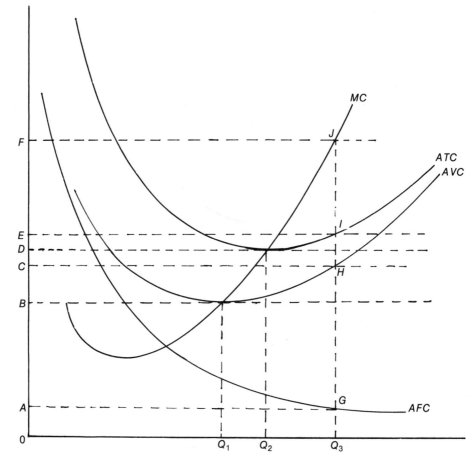

Quantity (output per day)

(a) At output level $0Q_3$ the total fixed cost is represented by the area $0AGQ_3$ or _____, the total variable cost is _____, and the total cost is _____.

(b) The short-run shutdown price is _____. The firm therefore would not produce a quantity of _____ or less.

(c) At price $0F$, the profit-maximizing output is _____; the total profit at that output level is _____; and total revenue is _____.

(d) At price $0D$, the profit-maximizing output is _____; the pure profit at that output level is _____. The firm is able to cover (none/some/all) of its fixed costs.

(e) Assume the firm is producing $0Q_2$ units and selling these at price $0D$. Suppose there is then an increase in the price of a raw material used by the firm. This will result in:
(an upward shift/a downward shift/no change) in the AFC,
(an upward shift/a downward shift/no change) in the AVC,
(an upward shift/a downward shift/no change) in the ATC, and
(an upward shift/a downward shift/no change) in the MC.
In the short run, the firm will produce ($0Q_2$/less than $0Q_2$/more than $0Q_2$), and will sell the output at price ($0D$/above $0D$/below $0D$).

The firm will realize (pure profit/normal profit only/a loss) at this output level in the short run.

(f) Would the increased price of raw materials ever cause the firm to shut down in the short run? _____. Explain. _____

_____

_____

(g) Again assume the firm is producing $0Q_2$ units and selling these at price $0D$. Suppose the government imposes a business tax that is a fixed sum regardless of how much the firm produces. This will result in:
(an upward shift/a downward shift/no change) in the AFC,
(an upward shift/a downward shift/no change) in the AVC,
(an upward shift/a downward shift/no change) in the ATC, and
(an upward shift/a downward shift/no change) in the MC.
In the short run, the firm will produce ($0Q_2$/less than $0Q_2$/more than $0Q_2$), and will sell the output at price ($0D$/above $0D$/below $0D$).

The firm will realize (pure profit/normal profit only/a loss) at this output level in the short run.

Would the business tax ever cause the firm to shut down in the short run? _____. Explain. _____

_____

_____

(h) Again assume an output of $0Q_2$ units and a price of $0D$ under the original cost conditions. Suppose the demand for this good decreases, such that the firm now faces a price of $0C$. Explain what effect, if any, this will have on the firm's output and profit. _____

_____

_____

Will this decrease in price to $0C$ cause the firm to shut down in the short run? _____. Explain. _____

_____

_____

2. The Coldcreek Canoe Co. once made some of Canada's best canvas-covered canoes. But alas, canoeists' preferences and relative prices changed strongly in favour of aluminum and fibreglass canoes. The fall in demand for canvas-covered canoes was so severe that the Coldcreek Canoe Co. and many small canoe firms like it could no longer make a normal profit in the long run. They discontinued the production of canoes and specialized in the production of high-quality canoe paddles.

Assume that the only costs in paddle production are the fixed costs of $2,000 per week for equipment rental and variable costs of $500 per week for each worker employed.

Assume also that a firm can employ a worker for less than a full week.

(a) Complete the following tables:

Table 17.1

Labour (no. of workers)	Output per Week (Total Product)	Average Product	Marginal Product
0	0	0	4
1	4	4	11
2	15	7.5	20
3	35	11.7	25
4	60	15	20
5	80	16	15
6	95	15.8	10
7	105	15	8
8	113	14.1	6
9	119	13.2	

Table 17.2

Labour (no. of workers)	Output per Week (Total Product)	Total Fixed Cost	Total Variable Cost	Total Cost	Marginal Cost	Average Fixed Cost	Average Variable Cost	Average Total Cost
0	0	2000	0	2000	125	—	0	—
1	4	2000	500	2500	45.45	500	125	625
2	15	2000	1000	3000	25	133.3	66.7	200
3	35	2000	1500	3500	20	57.1	42.9	100
4	60	2000	2000	4000	25	33.3	33.3	66.7
5	80	2000	2500	4500	33.3	25	31.25	56.25
6	95	2000	3000	5000	50	21.0	31.6	52.6
7	105	2000	3500	5500	62.5	19	33.3	52.4
8	113	2000	4000	6000	83.33	17.7	35.4	53.1
9	119	2000	4500	6500		16.8	37.8	54.6

(b) Plot the average product and marginal product schedules on Figure 17.2. The marginal product values are plotted midway between the quantity values (i.e. number of workers) to which each value refers. Join the values plotted to form smooth continuous curves and label them.

Figure 17.2

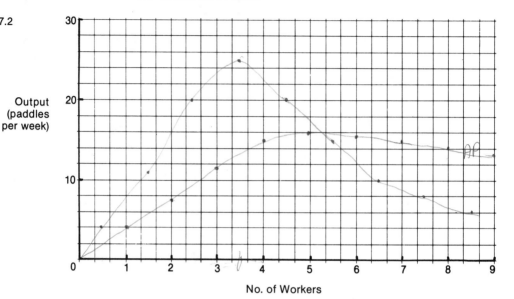

Output (paddles per week)

No. of Workers

(c) On Figure 17.3 plot the values calculated for marginal cost, average fixed cost, average variable cost, and average total cost. Again, plot the marginal values midway between the quantity values (i.e. output) to which each value refers.

(d) The *MC* curve is at a minimum at an output of _____ paddles per week. This output level is reached by employing _____ workers; this number of workers is associated with a marginal product (see Figure 17.2) of _____ paddles. (Note the relationship between the minimum of the *MC* curve and the maximum of the *MP* curve.)

Figure 17.3

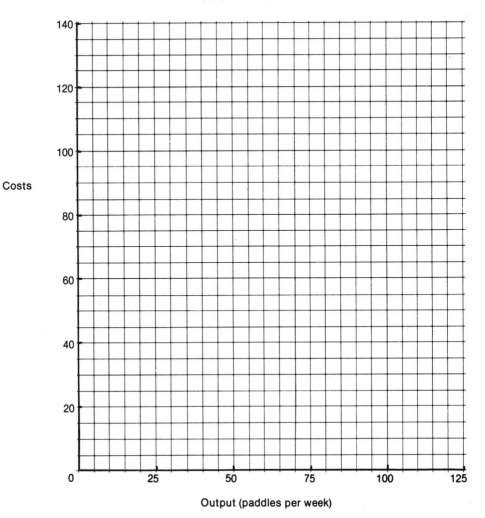

Costs

Output (paddles per week)

(e) The AVC curve is at a minimum at an output of _____ paddles per week. This output level is reached by employing _____ workers; this number of workers is associated with an average product (see Figure 17.2) of _____ paddles. (Note the relationship between the maximum of the AP curve and the minimum of the AC curve.)

(f) If the Coldcreek Canoe Co. operates under conditions of perfect competition, at a market price of $65 per paddle it will produce _____ paddles. At this weekly level of production it will make a (profit/loss) of approximately $_____.

(g) The firm will shut down if the market price of paddles is $_____ or less; but it will just make a normal profit if the price is $_____. At this price the firm will produce _____ paddles.

(h) Estimate the firm's short-run supply schedule by showing the number of paddles per week the firm would be willing to supply at each of the following prices: (Use the *MC* curve plotted on Figure 17.3).

Price:	$30	40	50	60	70	80
Quantity Supplied:						

(i) Suppose the market demand for paddles is as follows:

Price	$30	40	50	60	70	80
Quantity Demanded:	2,800	2,750	2,650	2,500	2,260	2,000
Quantity Supplied:						

If the Coldcreek Canoe Co. is one of 20 firms in the industry, and each firm has the same cost conditions, complete the supply schedule for the industry in the table above.

The equilibrium price for the paddle industry is $_____; the quantity sold at this price is _____; and at this price each firm will be making (a loss/normal profit only/some pure profit). Consequently, in the long run, the number of firms in the industry will tend to (increase/decrease/remain constant) and the price will tend to (increase/decrease/remain constant).

3. Given below are the average total costs for producing various quantities of widgets in plants of four different sizes.

(a) Complete the Long-Run Average Total Cost schedule in this table.

		Average Total Cost			Long-Run Average
Output	Plant 1	Plant 2	Plant 3	Plant 4	Total Cost
10	$110				$ 110
20	80				80
30	68				68
40	63	$100			63
50	65	65			65
60	70	47			47
70	83	39	$77		39
80		38	56		38
90		41	46		41
100		52	42	$73	42
110		76	44	58	44
120			51	51	51
130			69	51	51
140				55	55
150				67	67
160				90	90

(b) Plot the *ATC* for each of the four plants and the *LRATC* on Figure 17.4. Join the points plotted for each curve with smooth continuous lines to produce the short-run and long-run *ATC* curves. Label each curve.

Figure 17.4

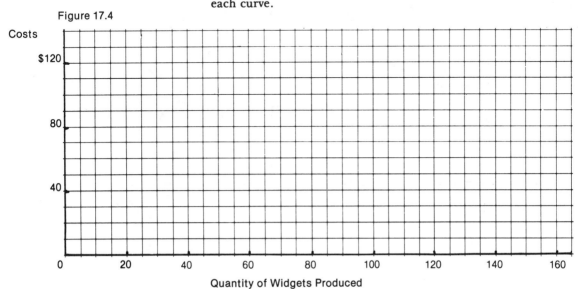

4. Assume that a firm in a perfectly competitive industry is in long-run equilibrium. Using diagrams, *show* and *explain* the effects on the firm's output, price, and profit, and on the *industry* price and output:

(a) when there is an increase in the wage rate for the unskilled labour used in this industry.

(i) in the short run:

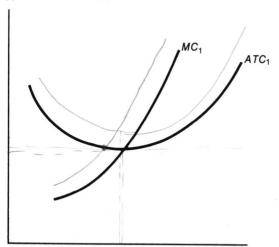
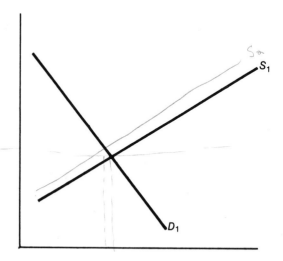

(ii) in the long run:

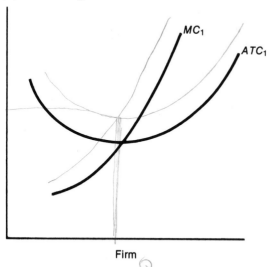
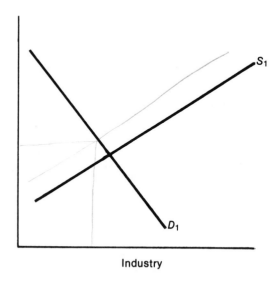

Firm

Industry

(b) when there is an increase in demand for the commodity produced
by this industry.

(i) in the short run:

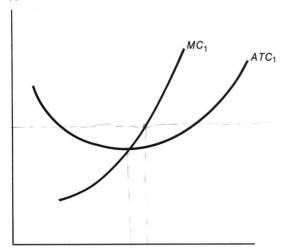
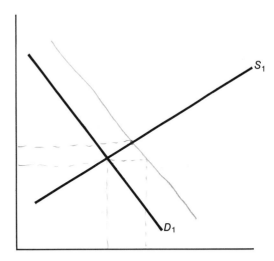

(ii) in the long run:

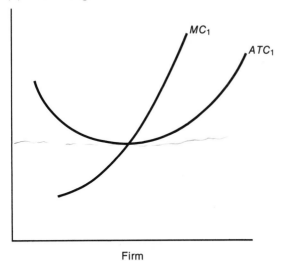
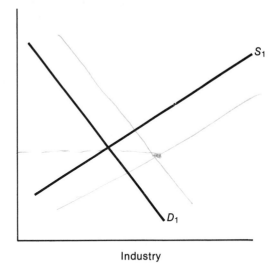

Firm   Industry

QUESTIONS FOR REVIEW AND DISCUSSION

1. "Since a perfectly competitive firm faces a perfectly elastic demand curve, each firm could produce an infinite quantity without affecting the market price." Do you agree? Explain.

2. Why does $P = MR$ for a perfectly competitive firm?

3. Are there any circumstances under which the MC curve would intersect the AVC curve at other than the minimum point of the AVC curve?

4. List the conditions that must be present for perfect competition to exist. Explain why the absence of any one of these conditions would result in less than perfect competition.

5. Explain carefully why the profit-maximizing (or loss-minimizing) output occurs where $MC = MR$.

6. An individual beef farmer does not advertise his product but the Canadian Cattlemen's Association may decide to advertise to encourage beef consumption. Is each acting rationally? Why? Use a supply and demand diagram to show the possible effects of advertising for the beef industry and for the individual farmer.

18   Monopoly and Imperfect Competition

IMPORTANT TERMS AND CONCEPTS

Be sure you can define or explain each of these terms before proceeding with the questions and problems.

imperfect competition
pure monopoly
oligopoly
monopolistic competition
barriers to entry
patent
natural monopoly
franchise
long-run marginal cost
monopolist's long-run equilibrium

monopoly power
price discrimination
perfect price discrimination
selling costs
interdependence of oligopolists
differentiated products
kinked demand curve
collusion (overt vs. tacit)
price leadership
non-price competition

MULTIPLE-CHOICE QUESTIONS

Circle the letter corresponding with the most appropriate answer for each question.

1. Which of the following statements is *incorrect*?

   (a) demand tends to be elastic at high prices and inelastic at low prices
   (b) in the price range where demand is elastic, marginal revenue is negative
   (c) demand is elastic if a price increase results in a decrease in total revenues
   (d) demand is of unitary elasticity at the price where total revenue reaches its maximum

2. A firm in a pure monopoly situation will find that:

   (a) marginal revenue cannot be negative
   (b) average revenue is equal to marginal revenue
   (c) average revenue is greater than marginal revenue at any level of output
   (d) marginal revenue increases as the price falls

3. A firm in a pure monopoly situation will also find that:

   (a) a pure profit can be made at any level of output
   (b) pure profit will be zero in the long run
   (c) pure profit can never be zero in the short run
   (d) pure profit can be positive, negative, or zero in the short run

4. Under conditions of perfect price discrimination, a monopolist will:

   (a) realize less profit than if all output were sold at the same price per unit
   (b) maximize profit by producing the output at which marginal cost is equal to average total cost
   (c) maximize profit by producing the output at which marginal cost is at a minimum
   (d) sell each unit at a different price, and in each case charge the highest price that a given consumer is willing to pay for that unit of the output

5. The oligopolistic firm faces a kinked demand curve on the assumption that:

   (a) other firms determine their prices in collusion with the given firm
   (b) other firms ignore a price cut but follow a price increase
   (c) all firms in the industry produce precisely the same product
   (d) other firms ignore a price increase but will follow a price cut

6. The price charged is greater than the marginal cost for firms in:

   (a) monopoly
   (b) oligopoly
   (c) monopolistic competition
   (d) each of the above

7. Product prices are likely to change least often under:

   (a) pure competition
   (b) pure monopoly
   (c) oligopoly
   (d) monopolistic competition

8. "Interdependence" in the case of an oligopoly means that:

   (a) each firm produces similar products
   (b) firms co-operate to keep new firms from entering
   (c) firms consider the possible reactions of competing firms when setting their product price
   (d) firms conduct very similar advertising programs

9. If all firms in an oligopoly were to practise explicit collusion, the resulting price and output would be similar to what would be observed if the industry were in:

   (a) pure competition
   (b) pure monopoly
   (c) price-discriminating monopoly
   (d) monopolistic competition

10. Monopolistically competitive firms:

    (a) realize normal profit in the short run, but a loss in the long run
    (b) realize normal profit in the short run and in the long run
    (c) realize either profit or loss in the short run, but tend to realize normal profit in the long run
    (d) realize pure or economic profit in the short and long run

11. The monopolistically competitive's firm's demand curve will tend to be more elastic:

    (a) the larger the number of firms selling similar products
    (b) the smaller the number of firms selling similar products
    (c) the greater the degree of product differentiation
    (d) the stronger the barriers to entry

12. Which of the following statements regarding a monopolistically competitive firm is *correct*?

    (a) the firm tends to make a normal profit in the long run because it produces at the minimum point on its *ATC* curve
    (b) the firm maximizes profit by producing where price equals marginal cost
    (c) in the long run the firm produces at an output level where average costs are rising
    (d) the firm faces a demand curve that at any given price is more elastic than that faced by a monopolist

TRUE/FALSE QUESTIONS

State whether each of the following statements is true or false, or whether you are uncertain because the statement may be either true or false depending on the relevant circumstances and/or assumptions. Explain the reasons for your answer in each case.

1. A monopoly will not maximize profit if it sells its product at a price where demand is inelastic.

2. When there are barriers to entry against potential competing firms, a monopoly will be assured of profits in the short run.

3. If a lump-sum subsidy were paid to every firm in monopolistic competition, the product price would not be affected in the short run.

4. The profit for a monopolistically competitive firm increases as its output increases.

5. Oligopolies with undifferentiated products are more likely to experience implicit collusion and price leadership than they are in the case of differentiated products.

6. A monopolist is not concerned about an increase in fixed costs because these can be passed on to customers through a price increase.

7. A monopolist is not concerned about increases in variable costs because these can be passed on to consumers through a price increase.

PROBLEMS

1. Assume that a monopolist has cost and revenue conditions as shown in the diagram below:

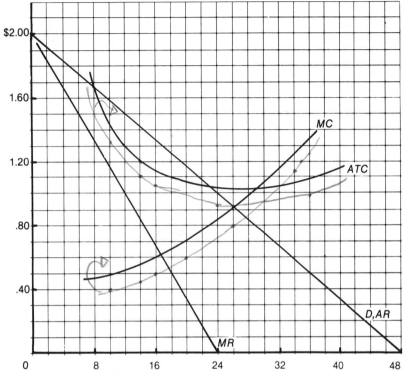

Output (millions of units per year)

(a) In order to maximize profit, the monopolist will produce _____ million units per year and will charge a price of _____ per unit. The firm's total revenue will be _____ per year. The maximum total revenue would occur at an output of _____ million units.

(b) The firm's average cost at its profit-maximizing level of output is $_____. The total cost at this output is $_____. The profit per unit is $_____, and the total profit is $_____.

(c) At any level of output between _____ and _____ million units, the monopolist will realize more than a normal profit.

(d) The monopolist's supply curve is _____ because

_____

_____

(e) Suppose now that the monopolist is required to install a pollution-control device in the plant at a cost of $5.1 million. Show the effect this would have on the firm's costs by drawing the new *MC* and/or *ATC* curve(s) on the diagram. The firm's profit-maximizing (or loss-minimizing) level of output would now be _____ million units per year. The firm would realize a (profit/loss) of $_____ per year.

(f) Suppose that, instead of requiring the firm to install the pollution-control device, the government imposes a pollution-removal tax of $.10 per unit produced. Show the effect this would have on the firm's costs by drawing the new *MC* and/or *ATC* curve(s) on the original graph. The firm's profit-maximizing (or loss-minimizing) level of output would now be _____ million units per year and the price charged would be $_____ per unit. The firm would realize a (profit/loss) of $_____ per year.

(g) Suppose the monopolist can practise perfect price discrimination (and that the government ignores the pollution problem). The profit-maximizing level of output would be _____ million units. The average cost would be $_____ and the total cost for this output would be $_____. The total revenue would be _____. Hence the profit under perfect discrimination is $_____, or $_____ greater than in the simple monopoly case as calculated in part (b) above.

2. The cost and revenue curves shown below are for Roma Pizza Palace, one of several pizza places surrounding the college campus in a large city. This would suggest that the firm is operating under conditions of monopolistic competition.

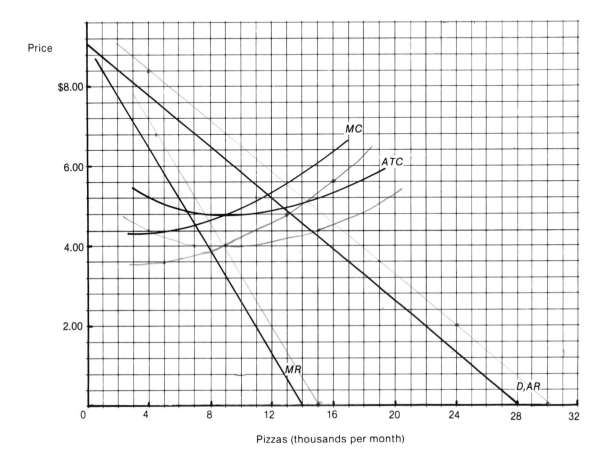

Pizzas (thousands per month)

(a) The restaurant will maximize its profit by producing _____ thousand pizzas per month and charging a price of $_____ per pizza. Since the average total cost for this output is $_____, the total profit will be $_____ per month.

(b) The restaurant knows that, since it and several other restaurants are realizing substantial profits, new restaurants may be opened in the area. Thus the Roma Pizza Palace decides to advertise by giving every customer a button stating "I eat at the Roma Pizza Palace". This adds 80¢ to the cost of every pizza produced, regardless of the level of output. However, this sales promotion also increases demand such that the quantity demanded at any price (up to $9.00) is increased by 2,000 pizzas per month.

Draw the new cost and revenue curves on the original graph and label the new curves. The new profit-maximizing level of output will be _____ thousand pizzas per month, and the price charged will be $_____. The average cost will be $_____ and the new total profit will be $_____ per month.

(c) Since the restaurant is still making a pure profit, other restaurants will be attracted to this area. The Roma Pizza Palace and other existing restaurants may incur increasing advertising costs, but they will also lose some sales to the new restaurants. Hence the demand will decrease and costs will increase until long-run equilibrium is reached. At this point $MC = (AC/MR/AR)$ and $AC = (MC/MR/AR)$ and pure profit is $_____.

QUESTIONS FOR REVIEW AND DISCUSSION

1. Why are there numerous retail automobile dealers but only a few automobile producers?

2. List several monopolistically competitive firms whose products you buy. What are the specific features of the products that led you to describe the firms as monopolistically competitive?

3. It has been claimed that advertising reduces product prices and also that it increases product prices. Could each claim be correct? Under what conditions?

4. "The greater the degree of interdependence among firms in an oligopoly, the greater will be the pressure for collusion among them." Do you agree? Why?

5. Would an increase in the size of the market (the number of potential buyers) for a particular commodity increase or reduce the degree of competition? Explain.

6. "Price discrimination increases monopolists' profits and therefore cannot be justified from the consumers' point of view." Explain why you agree or disagree.

19   Evaluation of Market Structures

IMPORTANT TERMS AND CONCEPTS

Be sure you can define or explain each of these terms before proceeding with the questions and problems.

efficiency   innovation
optimum rate of output   product variety
optimum scale   markup pricing
marginal cost pricing   theory of the firm

MULTIPLE-CHOICE QUESTIONS

Circle the letter corresponding with the most appropriate answer for each question.

1. For a firm in both pure competition and monopolistic competition:

   (a) price is equal to marginal cost
   (b) price is equal to marginal revenue
   (c) the quantity produced in the long run is at the point of minimum average total cost
   (d) pure profit in the long run is zero

2. "If the demand for commodity X increases, its price will increase." This is a reliable generalization:

   (a) with reference to the short run, assuming that X is produced in perfect competition;
   (b) with reference to the long run, assuming that X is produced in perfect competition;
   (c) with reference to the long run, assuming that X is produced by a monopoly;
   (d) with reference to the long run, assuming that X is produced in monopolistic competition.

3. The organizational structure of firms should be evaluated on the basis of:

   (a) efficient use of productive resources
   (b) innovation in products and techniques
   (c) both (a) and (b)
   (d) none of the above

4. The long-run profit-maximizing output of a monopolistically competitive firm, compared with a perfectly competitive firm facing the same cost conditions, will always be:

   (a) greater than under perfect competition
   (b) less than under perfect competition
   (c) equal to the output under perfect competition
   (d) unpredictable, without more information

5. A firm in perfect competition produces, in the long-run equilibrium, at its:

   (a) optimum scale of output
   (b) optimum rate of output
   (c) maximum profit
   (d) all of the above

6. When the price of the output is equal to its marginal cost:

   (a) the firm is producing below its optimum rate of output
   (b) consumer surplus is at a maximum
   (c) the firm must be realizing a loss
   (d) all of the above

TRUE/FALSE QUESTIONS

State whether each of the following statements is true or false, or whether you are uncertain because the statement may be either true or false depending on the relevant circumstances and/or assumptions. Explain the reasons for your answer in each case.

1. The demand curve facing a perfectly competitive firm tends to shift downward as the firm moves toward its long-run equilibrium position.

2. The monopolistically competitive firm makes a profit in the short run.

3. Given the same cost conditions, a monopolistically competitive firm produces less efficiently than does a perfectly competitive firm.

4. If a monopoly firm is realizing a profit in the short run, other firms will be attracted into this industry.

5. An oligopolistic firm usually faces the same conditions that prevail for a monopolistically competitive firm.

6. The optimum rate of output is the quantity at which a firm is maximizing profit or minimizing loss.

7. The incentive to innovate is greatest among perfectly competitive firms.

8. Product variety is likely to be greatest in the case of oligopolies.

PROBLEM

1. The diagrams below show the marginal cost curve for a single firm in a perfectly competitive industry, and the demand curve for the industry's output. There are 30 identical firms in the industry.

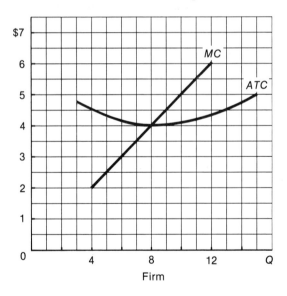

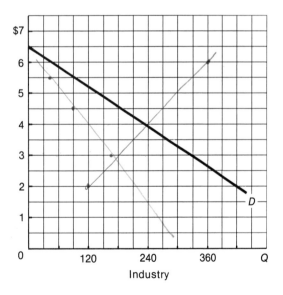

(a) Plot the industry's supply curve on the industry diagram. The equilibrium price in this market would be _____ per unit; the quantity sold would be _____ units.

(b) If the industry were to become a monopoly (through successive mergers and take-overs), but all cost and revenue conditions remained unchanged, the profit-maximizing output for the monopolist would be about _____ units, and the selling price would be about _____. (You will need to estimate these two values from the grid-lines of the graph.)

(c) The monopolist's price would be (higher/lower) than the competitive industry's price by _____ per unit, and the monopolist would produce _____ units (more/less) than the competitive industry.

(d) On the industry diagram, indicate the consumers' surplus under conditions of (i) perfect competition, and (ii) monopoly. (Use shading or cross-hatching to show these two areas.)

QUESTIONS FOR REVIEW AND DISCUSSION

1. If innovations, produced under conditions of imperfect competition, improve the efficiency in the use of resources, why should perfect competition continue to be an economic ideal?

2. Distinguish between innovation and product variety as desirable features of market structures. Which would you rate more highly, and why?

3. There are no cases of the perfectly competitive ideal in the real world, but are there any cases of monopolistic competition? Describe these carefully in terms of their product differentiation and freedom of entry.

4. Distinguish between optimum rate of output, optimum scale of plant, and profit-maximizing output. Are there any cases when the three concepts are coincident, that is, when a given level of output would be representative of each condition?

5. "The degree of excess capacity in a firm depends on the price elasticity of demand for its product." Do you agree? Why?

6. Explain carefully why $P = MC$ is a necessary condition for the most efficient use of resources.

20 Industrial Organization and Public Policy

IMPORTANT TERMS AND CONCEPTS

Be sure you can define or explain each of these terms before proceeding with the questions and problems.

industrial organization
industrial concentration
concentration ratio
single proprietorship
partnership
corporation
unlimited liability
limited liability
common stock
preferred stock
corporate bond
depreciation allowance
ownership vs. control

holding company
crown corporation
cooperative
Competition Act
restrictive trade practices
merger
natural monopoly
regulatory agency
"fair return"
National Transportation Agency
Canadian Radio-Television and
    Telecommunications
    Commission
National Energy Board

MULTIPLE-CHOICE QUESTIONS

Circle the letter corresponding with the most appropriate answer for each question.

1. The industrial concentration ratio:
   (a) refers to the number of establishments operated by a single firm
   (b) is highest in industries like household furniture and women's clothing
   (c) is a measure of the number of firms that account for most of the economic activity (sales, employment) in an industry
   (d) is greater in American manufacturing than in the Canadian manufacturing industry

2. Limited liability:

   (a) means that single proprietors are not financially responsible for more than the amount initially invested in the business
   (b) means that each person in a partnership is responsible only for his/her own financial contributions to the firm
   (c) means that persons who own part of a company are financially liable only for their share of the firm's net liability
   (d) means that firms are limited in their financial liabilities just as are individual persons

3. One of the sections of the Competition Act:

   (a) requires that existing monopolies be divided into smaller firms
   (b) has been effective in controlling the growth of large corporations
   (c) prohibits mergers and takeovers
   (d) prohibits manufacturers from enforcing the retail selling price of their products

4. A firm is described as a natural monopoly if:

   (a) it is technically impossible to establish a second firm in the industry
   (b) its average total costs continue to decline with increased output
   (c) it has a high degree of monopoly power
   (d) it is the price leader in its industry

5. The primary public objective in regulating a natural monopoly is to:

   (a) control the excessive profits such a monopoly could make in the absence of regulation
   (b) ensure that the monopoly always charges a price equal to its marginal cost
   (c) require that the monopoly charge the lowest possible price while just realizing sufficient profit to keep the monopoly in existence
   (d) encourage other firms to enter the industry to increase competition and hence lower the price of the commodity in question

6. A "fair rate of return" for regulated industries is considered to be about:

   (a) 4 per cent
   (b) 8 per cent
   (c) 12 per cent
   (d) 20 per cent

7. The principal federal regulatory agencies include all but the:

    (a) National Transportation Agency
    (b) Canadian Liquor Control Commission
    (c) Canadian Radio-Television and Telecommunications Commission
    (d) National Energy Board

8. Which of the following statements is *correct*?

    (a) the Competition Act restricts the growth of large firms in Canada
    (b) the patent system is one method governments use to increase competition in markets
    (c) a firm's size (in terms of sales or employees) is not necessarily a good indicator of the extent of its monopoly power
    (d) the smallest firms, when taken together, account for almost all of the total value of production in Canadian manufacturing

TRUE/FALSE QUESTIONS

State whether each of the following statements is true or false, or whether you are uncertain because the statement may be either true or false depending on the relevant circumstances and/or assumptions. Explain the reasons for your answer in each case.

1. The industrial concentration ratio presents an approximate measure of the degree of monopoly in an industry.

2. The effective control of a corporation requires that an individual or firm hold at least 51 per cent of the corporation's common shares.

3. The Competition Act gives the federal government the power to break up existing monopolies.

4. A natural monopoly exists if one firm owns all of the sources of the raw material used in its production process.

5. Regulatory agencies are intended to maintain the economic advantages of large scale while reducing price to bring it closer to what would prevail under more competitive conditions.

6. Public licensing of certain occupations or businesses is another method to increase competition.

PROBLEM

1. Suppose you have the following information concerning the carpet industry in Canada:

Firm	Value of Sales ($ millions)
A	15.0
B	7.0
C	2.0
D	1.0
E	0.5
F	0.3

(a) What is the concentration ratio in this industry, when concentration is defined as in Table 20.1 of the textbook? _____.

(b) Would you describe this industry as an oligopoly or monopolistic competition? _____

Why? _____

_____

(c) Suppose that firms B and D plan to merge. Is it likely that such a merger would be permitted within the terms of the Competition Act? _____. Why? _____

_____

_____

(d) If firms A, B, and E were to merge, would the industry then be an example of a natural monopoly? _____. Why? _____

_____

_____

QUESTIONS FOR REVIEW AND DISCUSSION

1. Would you prefer to hold financial assets in the form of corporate bonds, as common shares, or as preferred shares? Explain. Would your answer be different in a recession than at the peak of an economic expansion?

2. Why are corporations relatively more common in manufacturing than in retail services? Than in agriculture?

3. Discuss the uses and limitations of "concentration ratios" as a measure of industrial concentration.

4. Some economists have proposed that there should be more, rather than fewer, mergers in some industries in Canada. Why might they argue this way? Would you?

5. "All natural monopolies should be purchased by the government and be operated by a public commission." Do you agree? Why?

6. Do you think the patent system should be continued? Why or why not?

7. It is frequently suggested that urban public transportation should be provided at a lower price between 10 a.m. and 3 p.m. than during rush-hours. How should the lower price be determined? Do you agree with this proposal? Why?

21 Economics of the Natural Resource Industries

IMPORTANT TERMS AND CONCEPTS

Be sure you can define or explain each of these terms before proceeding with the questions and problems.

natural resource industries
price supports
offer to purchase
deficiency payments
hog cycle or cobweb theorem
marketing boards
production rights or quotas
rotation decision
rate of time preference
stumpage charges

maximum sustainable yield
200-mile limit
stinting rights
National Oil Policy
National Energy Program
domestic vs. world oil price
foreign ownership vs. foreign
  control
multinational corporations

MULTIPLE-CHOICE QUESTIONS

Circle the letter corresponding with the most appropriate answer for each question.

1. The existence of a "hog cycle" in agricultural production:
   (a) is found only in the case of pork production
   (b) will cause prices for the product concerned to fluctuate more widely, the less elastic is the demand for the product relative to the elasticity of supply
   (c) is due to seasonal changes in the demand for the product
   (d) can be moderated or controlled only by introducing production quotas

2. The deficiency-payments method for supporting farm prices requires larger government expenditures:
   (a) as the cost of transporting and storing goods increases
   (b) if, *ceteris paribus*, there is an increase in the demand for the farm product in question
   (c) the more inelastic is the demand for the farm product
   (d) the more elastic is the demand for the farm product

3. A policy of reducing the supply of a farm product by assigning production quotas will raise farm incomes only if:

(a) the demand for the product is inelastic
(b) the demand for the product is elastic
(c) farmers can also reduce their production costs
(d) the government buys any quantity produced in excess of the quota

4. Compared with prices of other goods and services, the prices of farm products, in the long run, tend to:

(a) decline
(b) increase
(c) remain constant
(d) display no consistent pattern

5. A major criticism of the quota system used by agricultural marketing boards is that:

(a) it could provide a capital gain when the quota is sold to another producer
(b) provincial quotas impede the efficiency of a national market
(c) higher costs of domestic production encourage the use of tariffs against importation of related products
(d) all of the above are true

6. Price support programs in agriculture provide:

(a) a specific subsidy per unit produced
(b) a guaranteed minimum price per unit produced
(c) a guaranteed price equal to the equilibrium price
(d) a guarantee that government will buy any amount not sold at the existing market price

7. The 200-mile limit refers to the coastal area within which:

(a) only Canadian boats can fish
(b) Canadian and foreign boats can fish, provided they have been assigned a quota
(c) fishing is controlled by reference to a maximum substainable yield
(d) none of the above

8. A major economic problem in the Canadian fishing industry is that:

(a) there are too few trawlers and fish plants
(b) there are too many trawlers and fish plants
(c) there is too little competition from foreign fishing
(d) the market for fish is strongly regulated by the fish marketing boards

9. Stumpage charges are the fees paid by logging companies to:

   (a) replace the trees that were harvested
   (b) remove the stumps remaining after harvest
   (c) the provincial governments, for trees harvested from crown lands
   (d) none of the above

10. A royalty, or tax, on the quantity or value of mineral production:

    (a) provides an unstable source of government revenue
    (b) can be designed to have a modest conservation effect
    (c) encourages efficient mining of all mineral deposits
    (d) is not commonly used in Canada

11. The National Oil Policy established the Ontario-Quebec boundary for differential oil policies. This resulted in:

    (a) higher oil prices in Quebec than in Ontario
    (b) subsidized use of natural gas in eastern Canada
    (c) higher tariffs on U.S. oil used in eastern Canada
    (d) Alberta oil being sold to the U.S. and imported oil being used in Quebec and the Maritimes

12. The National Energy Program of 1980 was designed to:

    (a) reduce imports of petroleum
    (b) increase Canadian ownership of the petroleum industry
    (c) redistribute the petroleum revenue among the oil companies, provincial governments, and the federal government
    (d) all of the above

13. Foreign ownership in Canadian industry:

    (a) has increased substantially relative to Canadian ownership in the past 10 years
    (b) is restricted by the Competition Act
    (c) is due partly to Canada's tariffs on manufactured goods
    (d) is especially predominant in the railways

TRUE/FALSE QUESTIONS

State whether each of the following statements is true or false, or whether you are uncertain because the statement may be either true or false depending on the relevant circumstances and/or assumptions. Explain the reasons for your answer in each case.

1. The deficiency-payments scheme for price supports requires larger government payments than when the offer-to-purchase scheme is used to maintain a given price level.

2. Restrictive production quotas are an effective method to increase farm incomes.

3. The cobweb theorem explains that fluctuations in the prices of agricultural commodities are due to changes in demand for the products during their production period.

4. The price elasticity of demand for farm products is generally less than 1.0.

5. Although prices are unstable in a "hog cycle", this is usually a temporary condition, with prices returning to the original equilibrium.

6. Provincial marketing boards administer price support programs to raise farm incomes.

7. The rotation decision in forestry management depends on the rate at which forests are harvested, compared with the rate at which they can be replaced by the logging industries.

8. Over 50 per cent of the fish caught by the Canadian fishing industry is used for domestic consumption.

9. The maximum sustainable yield of fish in a particular area is a reasonable guide in determining fishing quotas.

10. The Canadian government responded to the OPEC oil price increase in 1973 by raising the price of Canadian oil to the new world level.

11. There is not a "world price" for natural gas, comparable to the world price for oil.

PROBLEMS

1. The following data are for the price per 100 kg and quantity (thousands of kg) of potatoes sold over a period of six years (t_1 to t_6).

	t_1	t_2	t_3	t_4	t_5	t_6
P	\$11	$5\frac{1}{2}$	$8\frac{1}{2}$	7	8	$7\frac{1}{2}$
Q	2	16	7	12	10	11

(a) Plot these data on the diagram below, and draw in the "cobweb" pattern to show the lagged supply response to changes in price.

(b) Plot the changes in price on the right-hand diagram.

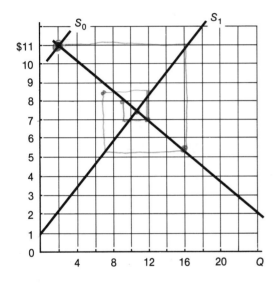 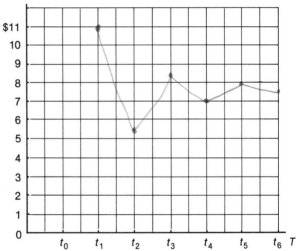

(c) How can you explain these fluctuations in price and quantity? _____

_____

_____

_____

_____

(d) If the demand were less elastic, would the fluctuations be greater or less? _____

If the supply were less elastic, would the fluctuations be greater or less? _____ Explain your answer for each case. _____

_____

_____

_____

_____

(e) The above fluctuation represents the potato market's reaction to an improvement in technology (such as better fertilizer) that caused the supply to shift from S_0 to S_1. Would a similar pattern of price fluctuation result from an increase in demand? _____

_____

_____

_____

_____

QUESTIONS FOR REVIEW AND DISCUSSION

1. Conservation of natural resources is a popular public issue, yet there is seldom consideration of how much conservation there should be. Discuss approaches that might be taken in determining the rate of depletion or use of these resources. Consider also the arguments against an extremist who proposes that, since these resources will be more valuable in the future, none should be taken now.

2. Why are the prices received by farmers less stable than the prices paid by farmers?

3. "The farm problem becomes worse the more government attempts to intervene. The only solution is to let the free market take its course." Explain carefully why you agree or disagree.

4. The cobweb theorem is often used to explain fluctuations in the prices of agricultural commodities. What examples can you think of in other industries where the cobweb theorem may be applicable?

5. List the advantages and disadvantages, for producers and consumers, of controlled or regulated prices for domestically produced oil; and of high versus low prices for oil.

6. The OPEC cartel set both the level of oil prices, and output quotas, at various times during the past two decades. Can it do both of these successfully? Why? Which approach would you recommend, and why?

7. The control of a major part of the Canadian petroleum industry lies in the United States. Do you think the public concern about foreign control would be lessened if this same degree of foreign control were distributed about evenly over four or five countries instead? Why?

PART FOUR

Distribution
of Incomes

22 Demand for Factor Services

IMPORTANT TERMS AND CONCEPTS

Be sure you can define or explain each of these terms before proceeding with the questions and problems.

factors of production
factor services
entrepreneurship
marginal productivity theory
marginal physical product
marginal revenue product

marginal resource cost
derived demand
profit-maximizing factor
   combination
cost-minimizing factor
   combination

MULTIPLE-CHOICE QUESTIONS

Circle the letter corresponding with the most appropriate answer for each question.

1. Marginal revenue product is defined as:

   (a) the increase in total resource cost associated with an additional unit of the production resource
   (b) the increase in total revenue associated with an additional unit of output
   (c) the increase in total revenue associated with an additional unit of the productive resource
   (d) the decrease in price required to sell an additional unit of the product

2. An increase in the demand for a productive factor's services will be caused by:

   (a) a decrease in the productivity of the factor
   (b) a decrease in the price of a substitute factor's services
   (c) an increase in the demand for the output produced by the factor
   (d) a decrease in the price of the given factor's services

3. The elasticity of demand for a factor's services will be greater:

(a) the more sharply its marginal product diminishes
(b) the less elastic is the demand for the product it produces
(c) the greater the number of close substitutes for the factor
(d) the smaller is the portion of total costs due to the given factor

4. Which of the following statements is *correct?*

(a) firms should employ productive factors until the total output of each is equal
(b) the marginal revenue product of a firm in pure competition declines solely because of diminishing marginal productivity of factors
(c) the more elastic the demand for a product, the less elastic will be the demand for the resources used to produce that product
(d) the more competitive the market in which a firm sells its product, the less elastic will be the firm's demand for productive factors

5. Marginal resource cost is defined as:

(a) the increase in total resource cost associated with an additional unit of the productive resource
(b) the increase in total revenue associated with an additional unit of output
(c) the increase in total revenue associated with an additional unit of the productive resource
(d) the decrease in price required to sell an additional unit of the product

6. The lowest-cost combination of factor services occurs when:

(a) marginal resource cost equals marginal revenue product
(b) marginal cost equals marginal revenue
(c) marginal resource cost is at a minimum
(d) the ratio of marginal physical product to marginal resource cost is equal for each factor

TRUE/FALSE QUESTIONS

State whether each of the following statements is true or false, or whether you are uncertain because the statement may be either true or false depending on the relevant circumstances and/or assumptions. Explain the reasons for your answer in each case.

1. The prices of factor services are major determinants of the distribution of income.

2. A firm should employ additional units of factor services if their price is less than their marginal revenue product.

3. A firm's demand curve for factor services is the same as the marginal product curve.

4. Marginal resource cost declines as the quantity of output increases.

5. The marginal revenue product for a firm is the additional revenue it receives for each additional unit sold.

6. The elasticity of demand for labour is determined partly by the elasticity of demand for the product of that labour.

PROBLEMS

1. Suppose that you are given the following information regarding the output a firm could obtain by employing various quantities of labour:

Labour (days)	Output per Day (Total Product)	Product Price	Total Revenue	Marginal Revenue Product
0	0	$8.80	_____	
1	15	8.00	_____	_____
2	28	7.20	_____	_____
3	39	6.40	_____	_____
4	48	5.60	_____	_____
5	55	4.80	_____	_____
6	60	4.00	_____	_____

(a) Complete the schedules for total revenue and for marginal revenue product.

(b) If the price of labour is $80 per day, how much labour will the firm employ? _____. If the price had been $44 per day, how much labour would be employed? _____.

(c) From the information given, it can be concluded that the firm is selling its product in a market that is (perfectly/imperfectly) competitive.

2. Assume that a firm is using both skilled labour and unskilled labour in such a combination that the marginal revenue product (MRP) of skilled labour is $80 and the MRP of unskilled labour is $30. If the price of skilled labour is $100 per unit and the price of unskilled labour is $25 per unit, the firm should employ (more/less/the same amount) of skilled labour and (more/less/the same amount) of unskilled labour.

3. Assume you are given the following information for a firm selling its product in a perfectly competitive market at $3.00 per unit:

Unskilled Labour			Skilled Labour		
Quantity Employed (hours)	MPP	MRP	Quantity Employed (hours)	MPP	MRP
1	25	————	1	40	————
2	20	————	2	36	————
3	15	————	3	32	————
4	10	————	4	24	————
5	5	————	5	20	————
6	2	————	6	16	————
7	1	————	7	8	————

(a) Complete the marginal revenue product schedules in the table provided.

(b) If the price of unskilled labour is $5 per hour and skilled labour is $8 per hour, the profit-maximizing combination of resources is ———— hours of unskilled labour and ———— hours of skilled labour.

(c) If the product price did not change but wages increased to $15 per hour for unskilled labour and $20 per hour for skilled labour, the profit-maximizing combination of labour would be ———— hours of unskilled labour and ———— hours of skilled labour.

QUESTIONS FOR REVIEW AND DISCUSSION

1. Distinguish carefully between a factor and factor services, using the concepts of stocks and flows. Why is factor service the relevant concept for an analysis of demand?

2. Why is the marginal productivity theory of demand for factor services a major part of the explanation for income distribution? What limitations do you see in using the marginal productivity theory as the only explanation for the distribution of incomes?

3. Why is entrepreneurship considered to be different from labour service, and what is its contribution to production?

4. Distinguish between the terms "marginal revenue" and "marginal revenue product". Why does marginal revenue product decline more quickly for an imperfectly competitive firm than for a firm in perfect competition, in the product market?

23   Labour Markets and Wages

IMPORTANT TERMS AND CONCEPTS

Be sure you can define or explain each of these terms before proceeding with
the questions and problems.

wages   labour force participation rate
earnings   demand for labour
gross earnings   monopsony
take-home pay   equalizing differences
money wages
real wages   **Appendix:**
piece rate
labour supply (short- and   labour vs. leisure
  long-run)   income vs. substitution effect
                                         backward-bending supply curve

MULTIPLE-CHOICE QUESTIONS

Circle the letter corresponding with the most appropriate answer for each
question.

1. The term "real wages" means:

   (a) wage payments plus fringe benefits
   (b) current wages adjusted for changes in the consumer price index
       since a specific year
   (c) the same as "take-home pay"
   (d) total earnings including payment for overtime, etc.

2. The labour force participation rate:

   (a) is the same for females as for males
   (b) depends primarily on changes in immigration
   (c) is a major factor determining the short-run supply of labour
   (d) is a measure of the extent of unionization

3. Long-run labour supply depends on all but:

   (a) immigration and emigration
   (b) birth and death rates
   (c) education and training
   (d) minimum wage legislation

4. If a firm sells its product in an imperfect product market:

   (a) it must also be hiring labour in an imperfect labour market
   (b) its demand for labour will be less elastic than if its product were sold in a perfectly competitive market
   (c) it must therefore be a monopsonist in the labour market
   (d) the wage rate it pays will be indeterminate

5. In a monopsonistic labour market, the firm will maximize profit by employing the quantity of labour at which:

   (a) the wage rate equals the marginal revenue product
   (b) the wage rate equals the marginal resource cost
   (c) the marginal resource cost equals the average resource cost
   (d) the marginal resource cost equals the marginal revenue product

Appendix:

6. A firm's demand for labour is determined by:

   (a) the quantity of output it can sell
   (b) the marginal revenue from the sale of its product
   (c) the number of persons required to operate the fixed factors
   (d) the marginal revenue product associated with the various levels of labour input

7. A backward-bending supply curve for labour:

   (a) is the result of the substitution effect outweighing the income effect at high wage rates
   (b) is the result of the income effect outweighing the substitution effect at high wage rates
   (c) is the result of diminishing marginal product of labour
   (d) is the result of workers who are indifferent between leisure time and real goods and services

TRUE/FALSE QUESTIONS

State whether each of the following statements is true or false, or whether you are uncertain because the statement may be either true or false depending on the relevant circumstances and/or assumptions. Explain the reasons for your answer in each case.

1. An employee's real wage may decrease even though her nominal or money wage increases.

2. The labour force participation rate measures the average number of hours worked per week by the total labour force.

3. An economy's long-run labour supply depends on its birth rate and death rate.

4. The marginal revenue product of workers could not be a constant value as the labour input increased, even under perfect competition.

5. A monopsonistic labour market is one in which there is only one buyer of labour services.

6. The marginal cost of hiring an additional worker is the wage rate that must be paid to attract him/her to the firm.

7. The supply of labour to a firm in a competitive product market could be the same as that for a firm in monopolistic competition.

8. When the marginal revenue product for labour hired by a firm in perfect competition is greater than the prevailing wage rate, the firm can increase its profit by hiring more labour.

Appendix:

9. The income effect of a wage increase outweighs the substitution effect in determining the number of hours of labour offered.

PROBLEMS

1. The labour supply curve facing a firm in an imperfectly competitive labour market is represented by the following labour supply schedule:

Wage Rate ($/hr.)	Quantity of Labour Supplied	Total Resource Cost	Marginal Resource Cost
$ 1	0	$_____	
2	1	_____	_____
3	2	_____	_____
4	3	_____	_____
5	4	_____	_____
6	5	_____	_____
7	6	_____	_____
8	7	_____	_____
9	8	_____	_____
10	9	_____	_____

(a) Calculate the missing values in the table above.

(b) Plot the labour supply curve and the marginal resource cost (*MRC*) curve on the graph below. (Note that the *MRC* values are plotted at the mid-points of the quantity axis.)

(c) The slope of the labour supply curve is _____, and the slope of the *MRC* curve is _____, or _____ times the slope of the supply curve.

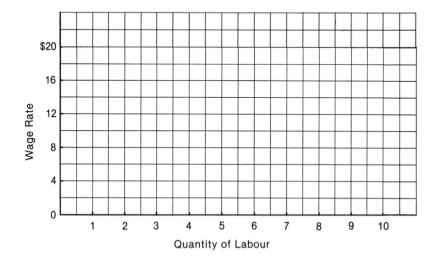

2. With reference to the diagram below, consider alternative labour market conditions, and the resulting wage rates and quantity of labour hired.

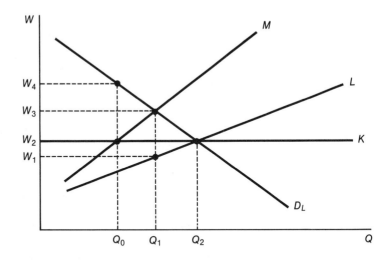

(a) In a perfectly competitive labour market, the supply curve facing an individual firm would be _____; the firm would employ _____ workers at a wage rate of _____.

(b) In an imperfectly competitive labour market, the supply curve could be represented by _____. In this case, the marginal resource cost of labour would be represented by _____. The quantity of labour hired would be _____ and the wage rate would be _____. In this case, workers would earn _____ less than under perfect competition, although the value of their marginal product would be _____.

QUESTIONS FOR REVIEW AND DISCUSSION

1. If there was perfect competition in all labour and product markets, would there still be wage differences among occupations? Explain.

2. What is meant by "derived" demand for labour? And how does this affect the price elasticity of demand for labour?

3. Distinguish between monopolists and monopsonists. Is it possible to be a monopolist but not a monopsonist, and vice versa? Describe examples of each case.

4. What is meant by the labour force participation rate? List as many reasons as you can for the increasing labour force participation rate for women aged 30 to 50.

5. Distinguish between a change in the demand for labour and a change in the quantity of labour demanded. What would cause each of these changes?

6. Describe or list some labour markets in your area in which short-run supply is fairly elastic, and others where supply is inelastic. Why do these differences exist?

7. Discuss all the reasons you can think of for higher incomes to be associated with higher levels of education. What examples can you suggest where a higher education may *not* increase one's income very much, if at all? Explain why these cases occur.

Appendix:

8. What impediments are there in the real world to the precise expression of a person's relative preference for labour income and leisure? Would most people you know in the labour force like to increase or decrease the number of hours they work per week, at the prevailing wage rates? Why?

24 Labour Unions and Collective Bargaining

IMPORTANT TERMS AND CONCEPTS

Be sure you can define or explain each of these terms before proceeding with the questions and problems.

craft union
industrial union
union goals
featherbedding
seniority
grievance procedures
union shop
open shop
closed shop

primary boycott
secondary boycott
collective bargaining procedures
certification
conciliation
compulsory arbitration
bilateral monopoly
industrial relations legislation

MULTIPLE-CHOICE QUESTIONS

Circle the letter corresponding with the most appropriate answer for each question.

1. Union membership as a percentage of the nonfarm labour force increased most rapidly:

   (a) during the Depression of the 1930s
   (b) during World War II
   (c) during the 1950s
   (d) during the 1960s

2. What percentage of union members in Canada are associated with international unions?

   (a) about 10 per cent
   (b) about 20 per cent
   (c) about 30 per cent
   (d) about 90 per cent

3. A closed shop is one in which:

   (a) union members have gone on strike
   (b) employers have locked out unionized employees
   (c) employers may hire only union members
   (d) new employees must join the union within 30 days

4. The specific objectives of unions include all but:

   (a) increasing wage rates
   (b) increasing fringe benefits
   (c) decreasing employers' profits
   (d) decreasing the length of the work week

5. The wage rate will be equal to the marginal revenue product of labour only if the labour market is:

   (a) a bilateral monopoly
   (b) a monopsony
   (c) imperfectly competitive
   (d) perfectly competitive

6. Which of the following statements is *correct?*

   (a) when the marginal revenue product of labour exchanged in a perfectly competitive labour market exceeds the wage rate, a firm should reduce the quantity of that labour it employs
   (b) more than one-half of all nonfarm paid workers in Canada now belong to labour unions
   (c) a union can legally go on strike as soon as its contract has expired and the union and management realize they disagree on the terms for the next contract
   (d) unions often attempt to increase the demand for union members' labour by urging the public to buy only union-made goods

7. If a labour market is one of bilateral monopoly, the wage rate will be:

   (a) established always at the wage that would prevail in perfect competition
   (b) established at the level desired by the employer
   (c) predictable only within a certain range
   (d) determined by the decisions of the union

8. Which of the following statements is *correct?*

   (a) unions can have no effect on the marginal physical product of labour

   (b) the short-run supply of labour varies with changes in the population's level of education and training

   (c) unions have been able to increase wages by about 30 per cent beyond what wages would have been in the absence of unions

   (d) as the percentage of the labour force with training in specific skills increases, this will, *ceteris paribus*, increase the wages of unskilled labour relative to the wages of skilled labour

TRUE/FALSE QUESTIONS

State whether each of the following statements is true or false, or whether you are uncertain because the statement may be either true or false depending on the relevant circumstances and/or assumptions. Explain the reasons for your answer in each case.

1. Craft unions can also be described as industrial unions.

2. Most of the unionized workers belong to international unions, which have their head offices in the United States.

3. All unions have the same goal: to raise the wage rate for their members.

4. A specific group of employees may belong to more than one union, and each union can then act as bargaining agent for the employees.

5. If a union and management cannot agree on a settlement, after a prescribed number of days of negotiation, the employees are then legally permitted to strike.

6. The overall impact of unions on the wage level differs among industries and regions.

7. Labour legislation in Canada is the exclusive responsibility of the provincial governments.

PROBLEMS

1. The diagram below shows the demand for labour for a firm operating a "3-minute car wash".

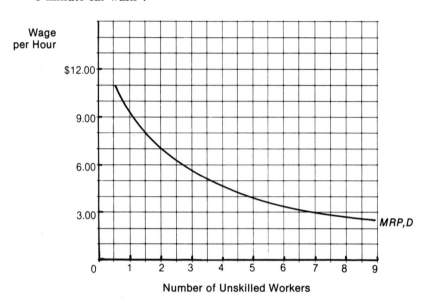

(a) Suppose the firm can employ any quantity of unskilled labour at $5.60 per hour. Draw the labour supply curve on this diagram.

(b) The firm will employ _____ workers at $5.60 per hour.

(c) Suppose the car wash workers in this city form a union and force the wage rate up to $7.00 per hour. The firm will now employ _____ workers. If they work 40 hours per week, the total weekly wage payments are (more/less) than the weekly wage payments prior to unionization by $_____ per week. This indicates that the demand for unskilled workers in the car wash firm is (elastic/unitary/inelastic).

(d) If the car wash workers' union can persuade other unions to require that all labour contracts have a clause specifying that company cars must be washed only at a unionized car wash, this will (increase/decrease/have no effect on) the demand for car wash workers in the above diagram. Consequently the car wash will employ (more/fewer/the same number of) workers at the $7.00 per hour union wage, and the total wage payments will (rise/fall/remain unchanged). The elasticity of demand at $7.00 per hour is now (greater than/less than/the same as) the elasticity before the inter-union agreements.

2. The diagram below shows the supply of and demand for labour for a single firm.

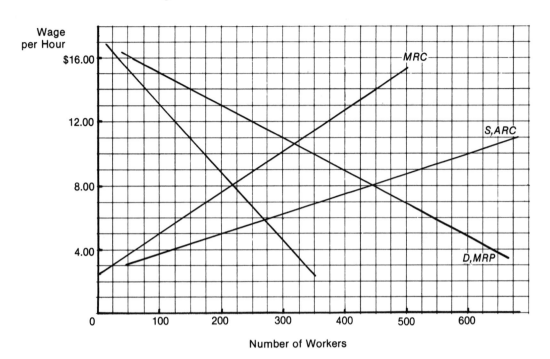

(a) The firm is facing a/an (perfectly competitive/imperfect) labour market because _____

_____

_____

(b) If workers in this labour market are not unionized, the firm will hire _____ workers at a wage rate of $_____ per hour. The marginal revenue product at this level of employment is $_____. Hence workers receive (more than/less than/the same as) their marginal revenue product.

(c) If this is the only firm labour in question and the workers form a union, the case becomes one of (monopoly/monopsony/bilateral monopoly). The union's objective would be to obtain a wage of $_____, while the employer would be willing to offer only $_____. The resulting wage will depend on _____

_____

_____

If the wage arrived at is $8.00 per hour, this is the same that would occur under conditions of _____

_____

_____

QUESTIONS FOR REVIEW AND DISCUSSION

1. Why have labour unions been formed mainly in the blue-collar occupations?

2. What factors determine how high a trade union can push wages without reducing the level of employment?

3. Many unions are opposed to increased mechanization in their industries, yet the existence of strong unions can hasten the rate at which firms mechanize their operations. How can you explain this?

4. Should persons employed in essential services such as police and fire protection have the right to strike? Why?

5. Featherbedding, seniority system, grievance procedure, work rules: what do these terms mean and what effect do you think each has on the efficient use of labour resources?

25 Rent, Interest, and Profit

IMPORTANT TERMS AND CONCEPTS

Be sure you can define or explain each of these terms before proceeding with the questions and problems.

transfer earnings
economic rent
quasi-rent
capital
present value of assets
internal rate of return
marginal value of assets
marginal efficiency of capital

nominal vs. real rate of interest
capital widening
capital deepening
structure of interest rates
time to maturity
profit
risk and uncertainty

MULTIPLE-CHOICE QUESTIONS

Circle the letter corresponding with the most appropriate answer for each question.

1. If a tax were levied on the economic rent from a piece of land:

    (a) the tax would cause the landowner to change the use of the land
    (b) the tax would not cause the landowner to change the use of the land
    (c) the tax would cause the landowner to sell the land
    (d) the tax would make it impossible for the landowner to sell the land because no one would want it

2. Economic or pure rent is:

    (a) payment to productive resources whose supply is perfectly elastic
    (b) that part of the payment to productive resources due to supply not being perfectly elastic
    (c) payment for the use of houses and apartments
    (d) salaries paid to celebrities in theatre and sports

3. Suppose that A.B.C. Co. is considering the purchase of a $100,000 machine. It should purchase the machine if:

(a) the present value is less than $100,000
(b) the present value is greater than $100,000
(c) the present value is exactly equal to $100,000, but not if the market rate of interest is unusually low
(d) the present value is equal to $100,000, but the salvage value is zero

4. The "structure of interest rates" refers to:

(a) the different net present values calculated for different capital goods
(b) the various interest rates associated with different kinds of financial assets
(c) the various interest rates banks charge to different categories of borrowers
(d) the changes that have occurred in interest rates over the past several years

5. In calculating the present value of a capital asset, the discount or interest rate used in the calculation should be:

(a) the best alternative rate of return on another asset
(b) the current interest rate on government bonds
(c) the current interest rate paid for savings deposits
(d) the internal rate of return for the asset in question

TRUE/FALSE QUESTIONS

State whether each of the following statements is true or false, or whether you are uncertain because the statement may be either true or false depending on the relevant circumstances and/or assumptions. Explain the reasons for your answer in each case.

1. Transfer earnings represent the payment required to attract a factor service away from its alternative uses.

2. If the supply of a factor service were perfectly elastic, there would be no economic rent component in its price.

3. The price paid for the use of land, commonly called "rent", depends primarily on the market value of the land.

4. The economic rent on land increases as demand for the use of that land increases.

5. Interest rates are based almost entirely on the estimated risk that the borrower will default on the loan.

6. The present value of a capital asset could only decrease in real terms in subsequent years.

PROBLEM

1. The labour market conditions for a professional hockey player are illustrated by the diagram below. The supply curve (*S*) indicates that the person will not play hockey for less than $20,000 per year. Between $20,000 and $80,000 per year, the player is willing to spend an increasing amount of time at hockey, and less time at other work or leisure. At a salary of $80,000 or more, the player will spend the full year playing hockey.

(a) What is the equilibrium salary for this player? _____

(b) On the graph, show how much of this salary is transfer earnings, and how much is economic rent.

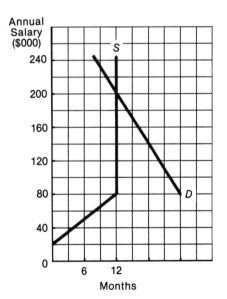

(c) If the government imposed a tax of $100,000 per year on this player, what would be the effect on supply or demand? Would the player still play for the full year, after the tax was imposed? Why?

(d) How large could the tax be without affecting the player's willingness to play hockey?

QUESTIONS FOR REVIEW AND DISCUSSION

1. Suppose that an area of residential land is rezoned for commercial uses. What change, if any, will there be in the economic rent realized on this land? Should any public action be taken concerning changes in economic rent resulting from zoning changes?

2. Why is the interest rate such an important price in the market system?

3. How can one account for the wide range of interest rates that occur at any given time in the economy?

4. "Normal profits, by definition, are enough to keep a firm in a given industry. The government should therefore tax away all profits in excess of normal profits." Do you agree? Why?

26 Income Distribution in Canada

IMPORTANT TERMS AND CONCEPTS

Be sure you can define or explain each of these terms before proceeding with the questions and problems.

functional income distribution
size distribution of income
Lorenz curve
poverty
poverty line
poverty rate
incidence of poverty
distribution of poverty
working poor

lost output
diverted output
Old Age Security Act
Canada Pension Plan
Canada Assistance Plan
National Housing Act
Unemployment Insurance Act
guaranteed annual income
negative income tax

MULTIPLE-CHOICE QUESTIONS

Circle the letter corresponding with the most appropriate answer for each question.

1. The functional distribution of income shows:

   (a) the relative shares of wages, profits, etc., in the national income
   (b) the percentage of the population at various income levels
   (c) the distribution of income received as transfer payments
   (d) the income distribution among various occupations

2. For several years in Canada the 20 per cent of the population receiving the highest incomes have received about what percentage of the total income?

   (a) 10
   (b) 20
   (c) 40
   (d) 60

3. The distribution of family income in Canada in recent decades:

(a) has tended to become more unequal
(b) has moved strongly toward greater equality
(c) has shifted in favour of the richest and poorest groups at the expense of the middle groups
(d) has become only slightly less unequal

4. Income inequality in Canada is partly explained by each of the following factors, with the exception of:

(a) age
(b) education and training
(c) number of weeks worked per year
(d) negative income tax

5. The calculation of a specific value for "the poverty line" is based on:

(a) the income level below which one finds 20 per cent of the population
(b) a survey of what Canadians believe to be the "minimum acceptable standard"
(c) an amount equal to the total transfer payments an unemployed head of a family of four would receive under the Canada Assistance Plan
(d) the income level at which families spend about 60 per cent or more of their income on food, shelter, and clothing

6. According to a Statistics Canada report, the poverty line in 1988 for a family of 4 living in a large city was about:

(a) $10,000
(b) $15,000
(c) $24,000
(d) $32,000

7. The poverty rate in Canada:

(a) is the same thing as the poverty line
(b) is the percentage of the population living on an income below the poverty line
(c) has fallen sharply in the past two decades
(d) is highest in British Columbia

8. For families that were below the poverty line in Canada in 1988, which of the following statements is *correct?*

   (a) about 25 per cent lived in the Atlantic provinces
   (b) about 50 per cent lived in cities
   (c) about 35 per cent were headed by a female
   (d) about 45 per cent were headed by a person aged 35 to 44

9. Which of the following statements is *correct?*

   (a) in Canada in recent decades the poor have become poorer and the rich have become richer
   (b) the negative income tax proposal is a means for administering a guaranteed annual income within the personal income tax system
   (c) unemployment compensation is financed entirely by contributions the government requires of employers
   (d) the majority of heads of families below the poverty line are unemployed

10. The negative income tax system:

    (a) does not create work incentives for low-income persons
    (b) can be considered a regressive tax system
    (c) simply is a system to exempt the poor from paying income tax
    (d) would replace most or all of the welfare transfer payment programs

11. An important feature of the negative income tax system is that if a low-income family could increase its employment income, the negative tax payment would be:

    (a) reduced by this amount
    (b) reduced by some fraction of this amount
    (c) unchanged
    (d) increased by this amount

TRUE/FALSE QUESTIONS

State whether each of the following statements is true or false, or whether you are uncertain because the statement may be either true or false depending on the relevant circumstances and/or assumptions. Explain the reasons for your answer in each case.

1. Labour income is the second-largest share in the functional distribution of income.

2. The percentage of the Canadian population living below the poverty line has dropped significantly during the past 25 years.

3. Poverty in Canada is concentrated in Quebec and the Prairie provinces.

4. Poverty is not caused solely by a lack of work; there are also substantial numbers of employed persons living below the poverty line.

5. Government grants to assist families in poverty have no long-run benefit because they remove the work incentive.

PROBLEM

1. Suppose that an economy has the following distribution of income:

Gross Income Level	Number of Persons at This Level	Total Income Received by Persons at This Level	Percentage of Economy's Total Income Received at This Level	Percentage of Population Who Are at This Income Level
$ 1,000	6	_____	_____	_____
3,000	18	_____	_____	_____
5,000	20	_____	_____	_____
8,000	33	_____	_____	_____
12,000	8	_____	_____	_____
20,000	9	_____	_____	_____
50,000	6	_____	_____	_____
Totals	100		100.0	100.0

(a) Complete the three remaining columns of data in the table above.

(b) Use this table to construct a Lorenz curve for the income distribution in this economy, on the graph below, and label the curve.

(c) Assume that the personal income tax rate is 20 per cent of gross income at each income level. Construct the Lorenz curve showing the resulting after-tax income distribution and label the curve.

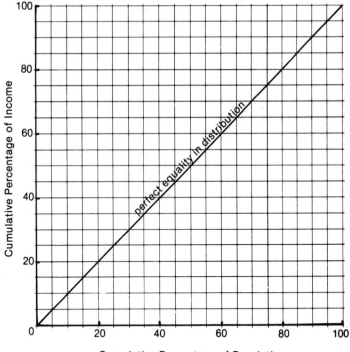

(d) Assume *alternatively* that there is a progressive personal income tax structure as shown in the table below:

Gross Income Level	Average Tax Rate (tax as a percentage of total income)	After-Tax Income	Number of Persons at This Level	Total Income Received by Persons at This Level	Percentage of Economy's Total Income Received at This Level
$ 1,000	0	_____	6	_____	_____
3,000	10	_____	18	_____	_____
5,000	15	_____	20	_____	_____
8,000	20	_____	33	_____	_____
12,000	25	_____	8	_____	_____
20,000	30	_____	9	_____	_____
50,000	35	_____	6	_____	_____
Totals	_____	_____	100	_____	100.0

Complete the remaining columns of data in the table.
Construct the Lorenz curve showing the after-tax income distribution that results from this tax structure, and label the new curve.

(e) How do different income-tax structures influence after-tax income distribution? What implications are there for public policy? _____

_____

_____

QUESTIONS FOR REVIEW AND DISCUSSION

1. What is the difference between the functional and personal distribution of income? How are these two concepts related?

2. Do you think the existing distribution of income in Canada is equitable)? Why? If not, use a Lorenz curve to describe the distribution you believe is equitable. Outline the programs you would advocate to achieve this result. If you think the existing distribution is equitable, what steps must be taken to maintain this distribution?

3. Think of two persons whose incomes you know are quite different. List as many reasons as you can for the difference in their incomes.

4. Develop a definition of poverty without including the general concept of a poverty line as described in this chapter. What difficulties do you encounter in devising such a definition?

5. Can the war against poverty ever be won? Explain. Outline what you believe to be the most effective anti-poverty programs, in light of the data provided on the incidence and distribution of poverty.

6. Some people are in favour of modifying the existing welfare system and increasing the amounts paid, others favour a reduction in welfare payments, while still others favour a negative income tax. Decide which position you favour and outline the arguments supporting your position and opposing the other positions.

27 Regional Income Disparity

IMPORTANT TERMS AND CONCEPTS

Be sure you can define or explain each of these terms before proceeding with the questions and problems.

regional income disparity
industrial composition
equalization payments

MULTIPLE-CHOICE QUESTIONS

Circle the letter corresponding with the most appropriate answer for each question.

1. The average annual income of income-earners in Canada in 1989 was about:

   (a) $14,000
   (b) $22,000
   (c) $30,000
   (d) $38,000

2. With respect to which of the following factors — as determinants of per capita income — do the Atlantic provinces find themselves in a *more* favourable position than the national average?

   (a) age composition
   (b) labour force participation rate
   (c) unemployment rate
   (d) industrial composition

3. Regional income differences in Canada are partly explained by:

   (a) age composition of the region
   (b) different unemployment rates
   (c) differences in the level of schooling
   (d) all of the above

4. Which of the following policies have *not* been used to encourage economic development in the Atlantic provinces?

(a) federal subsidies for freight rates
(b) monetary policy
(c) labour supply (or manpower) policies
(d) federal grants for investment in designated areas

TRUE/FALSE QUESTIONS

State whether each of the following statements is true or false, or whether you are uncertain because the statement may be either true or false depending on the relevant circumstances and/or assumptions. Explain the reasons for your answer in each case.

1. Average personal incomes in the Atlantic provinces are below the national average due mainly to the industrial composition of this area.

2. There has been very little change in the relative personal income per capita in the richest and poorest provinces during the past three decades.

3. Regions that have a high capital stock per worker also have a high capital/output ratio.

4. Equalization payments are an important mechanism used by the federal government to reduce interprovincial disparity in tax revenues.

5. Fiscal and monetary policies can be effective means to reduce regional income differences.

6. Tariff policies have been less effective than originally expected in the development of the Atlantic provinces.

QUESTIONS FOR REVIEW AND DISCUSSION

1. Average earnings in Ontario are among the highest in Canada, yet Canada's manufacturing industry is also concentrated in Ontario where labour costs are so high. Why do not more manufacturing firms locate in the lower-wage provinces?

2. It is sometimes suggested that the only way to reduce regional income disparity is to encourage the migration of people from the low-income areas to the high-income areas. What effect would this have on incomes in each area? Would the income change be greater if it were the most educated or least educated people who moved? Who is not likely to migrate in response to a general government offer of financial assistance for migration? Why?

3. If it is not possible to move people to areas where the jobs are, how can businesses be encouraged to move the jobs to areas where the people are? How would a government official weigh the benefits and costs of such a program?

Answers

CHAPTER 1

Multiple-Choice   1. c   2. b   3. b   4. d   5. b   6. c
7. d   8. c   9. a   10. d

True/False

1. False; intermediate goods require further processing before they can be used as either consumer or producer goods. The latter are final goods that may be used to produce either consumer goods or other producer goods.

2. False; the "fact of scarcity" means that there are not enough resources to satisfy everyone's wants, at no cost.

3. False; opportunity cost is defined in terms of the actual satisfaction or output that is given up by making the choice in question.

4. False; the new wheat variety will reduce the opportunity cost for wheat but increase the opportunity cost for cheese, at any given level of output of either cheese or wheat. Moreover, nothing can reduce the *relative* costs of *both* of any two commodities.

5. True; because the reduction in resources required to produce a given quantity of the good may be used to produce the other good.

6. True; a reduction in productive resources (such as net emigration of population) may reduce the production possibilities.

7. False; the boundary is based on the assumption of full employment (and most efficient technology).

8. Uncertain; this would be true if the economy were on its production-possibilities boundary; but false if it were inside the boundary, or if new resources or improved technology were available.

9. True; all economies face the problems or decisions of what, how, and for whom to produce, and under what rates of growth and resource use.

10. Uncertain; there are faults in each system that may be overcome by combining these systems in a "mixed economy".

Problems   1. (a)

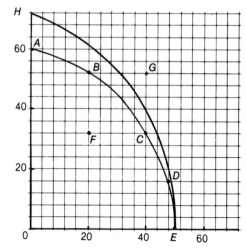

Consumer Goods (units per week)

(b) approx. 1.5 for 41st unit (2 over range C to D, 1 over range B to C); increases

(c) remain constant

(d) faster

(e) F

(f) 20

(g) impossible

(h) (i) inward

(ii) outward

(iii) outward

(iv) no change

(v) inward

(i) new curve is EH on diagram above. Yes, it can produce approximately 44 units of consumer goods, because the more efficient use of resources for producer goods production releases resources for producing consumer goods.

2. (a) $x_3 y_3$

(b) $x_3 y_2$

(c) $x_2 y_2$

(d) $x_2 y_2$

(e) $x_3 y_3$

CHAPTER 2

Multiple-Choice   1. c   2. c   3. b   4. c   5. b   6. c
                     7. c

True/False   1. True; an economic theory is valid if it can explain and predict the substantial majority of events to which it is addressed.

2. False; although individuals differ in many respects, they also tend to behave similarly in other respects, and particularly in their economic decisions.

3. False; economists generally agree on basic theory and empirical findings. But theory and policy are improved by discussions of disagreements about specific issues.

4. True; each of these components is essential in developing a complete theory.

5. False; the study of economics is also subject to scarce resources; not all topics can be studied with equal intensity.

6. False; economists do not have physical laboratories but they have libraries, data collection systems, and computer facilities, for the development of theory and analysis.

7. False; this assumption is important precisely because the economic environment does change.

Problem   1. (a) F   (b) S   (c) S
                (d) F   (e) F   (f) S

CHAPTER 3

Multiple-Choice   1. a   2. c   3. b   4. b   5. d   6. c
                     7. c   8. a   9. a   10. c   11. b   12. c
                    13. b   14. d   15. a

True/False   1. False; one cannot draw this conclusion unless it is known or assumed that the change was due only to a supply decrease with no change in demand.

2. Uncertain; the elasticity will certainly decrease if there is no change in the slope of the supply curve, but otherwise the elasticity could change in either direction.

3. False; a perfectly elastic (horizontal) demand curve does not.

4. False; if a supply curve were to intersect the quantity axis it would imply that a commodity would be supplied at zero price.

5. False; the demand for inferior goods would decrease.

6. Uncertain; a decrease in supply could more than offset the increase in demand (due to increased incomes).

7. True; the increase in price more than offsets the effect on revenue of the decrease in quantity.

8. True; but only for a perfectly inelastic demand curve.

9. Uncertain; the statement is true with the exception of a straight line through the origin and the extreme cases of perfectly elastic and perfectly inelastic supply.

10. False; inferior goods are those with income elasticity less than zero.

Problems

1. (a)

Figure 3.1

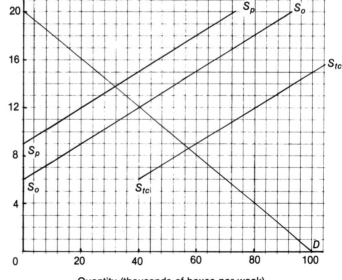

Price ($ per box)

Quantity (thousands of boxes per week)

(b) $12; 40,000
(c) Demand elasticity: .11, .33, .54, .82, 1.22, 2.33, 9.0
   Supply elasticity: −, −, 7.0, 3.15, 2.13, 1.77, 1.46
(d) remain constant; decrease
(e) $10; $20; $0
(f) new curve is labelled S_{tc}; $8.50; 57,000
(g) $480,000: $484,000
(h) less elastic; yes; $\Delta Q/\Delta P$ is unchanged but P/Q or
   $(P_1 + P_2)/(Q_1 + Q_2)$ decreases
(i) new curve is labelled S_p; $13.70; 32,000

2. (a)   −   0   −   −
   (b)   0   +   −   +
   (c)   +   0   +   +
   (d)   +   0   +   +
   (e)   +   0   +   +
   (f)   0   −   +   −

CHAPTER 4

Multiple-Choice

1. a	2. b	3. d	4. a	5. d	6. c
7. d	8. c	9. d	10. c	11. c	12. d
13. c	14. d	15. b	16. d		

True/False

1. False; various imperfections in the market system may result in ineffi-cient use of resources.

2. True; pure public goods would be available to anyone, so no one will individually undertake their production.

3. False; the greater the elasticity, the greater the reduction in quantity sold and the lower the tax revenue.

4. Uncertain; the price increase is equal to the tax only in the case of perfectly inelastic demand. In other cases, the price increase is less than the tax.

5. False; imposing a floor price does not affect supply or demand, and so does not affect equilibrium price.

6. False; lagged adjustments refer to changes in supply or demand, but externalities are effects ignored by both the supplier and the buyer.

7. Uncertain; an increase in the wage will, *ceteris paribus*, cause unemployment but total income will increase only if demand for labour is inelastic.

8. True; rent controls reduce the quantity of apartments available, so that there is an increased demand for houses and an increase in housing prices.

Problems

1. (a) none; none; fall; $60,000 [$480,000 − 420,000]; surplus; approx. 24,000 boxes
   (b) new supply curve lies below and parallel to original supply curve by a vertical distance equal to $4; approx. $9.60; approx. 51,000; $204,000 [$4 × 51,000]; no; no; $160,000 [$4 × 40,000]; 264,000 [$4 × 66,000]

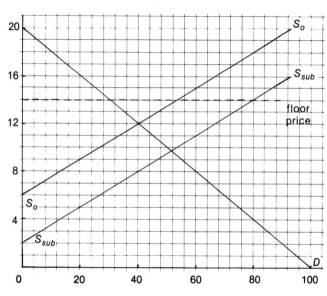

Figure 4.1

Price ($ per box)

Quantity (thousands of boxes per week)

2. (a) $14; 10,000; $140,000
   (b) D_1 (or D_2, since at zero price the quantity is the same for both curves) and S_1; the price to the consumer is now $0 with a resulting movement along the demand curve. There is no change in demand or in supply.
   20,000; $24; $480,000
   (c) 15,000; $19; $285,000
   (d) 11,000; $15; $165,000
   (e) $8; 18,000; $144,000; $140,000

3. (a) $1.50; 200; 0.6; 1.0
   (b) $1.20; 225; $112,500 (Draw the new supply curve and then estimate the *P* and *Q*.)
   (c) $2.60; decrease; $40,000; elastic; 1.24 (Estimates may vary slightly, depending on how carefully you have drawn the new supply curves.)

4. (a) $2.00
   (b) percentage; 50
   (c) 1.0; 0.82
   (d) increase; positive (if margarine is a substitute)
   (e) greater than
   (f) quantity supplied falls to 10; quantity demanded increases to 14
   (g) impose rationing on butter; offer subsidies to increase the supply of butter

5. (a) 0.5; 1.5
   (b) It takes time for potential riders to adjust to the change in relative prices, that is, for riders to switch from cars, as they become familiar with the quality and regularity of transit service.

CHAPTER 5

Multiple-Choice

1. d	2. d	3. b	4. c	5. d	6. b
7. a	8. d	9. c	10. b	11. d	12. b
13. b	14. b	15. d	16. d	.	.

True/False

1. True; the interest rate on a debt would have included the expected higher inflation rate.

2. False; the weights used in the CPI are likely more representative of parents than students.

3. True; increased costs for labour or other inputs are more easily passed on in more monopolistic labour and product markets.

4. False; even when wage rate increases exceed productivity increases, cost-push inflation might be avoided if competitive pressures lead to technological adjustments and/or profit reductions.

5. True; value added includes payments to all factors of production, including the firm's profit, which is calculated by subtracting other factor payments from the selling price.

6. False; GDP can be obtained by either approach because payments to productive factors must be equal to the value of final goods and services (after adjustments for indirect taxes and subsidies).

7. False; the difference between GNP and GDP is in the international payments of investment income.

8. True; Personal Income includes investment income (rent, interest, dividends), net income of unincoporated businesses, and transfer payments.

9. Uncertain; gross investment is usually greater than net investment, but if depreciation were zero (an extremely unlikely case) the two measures would be equal.

Problems

1. A 175, 15, 25, 20, 50
   B 145, 125, 35, 10
   C 155, 145, 135, 95

2. (a) I   (b) E   (c) N   (d) N
   (e) N   (f) E   (g) E   (h) I
   (i) I   (j) N   (k) I   (l) E

3. Yes, if the decrease in inventories is greater than new construction and equipment (which is highly unlikely although logically possible).
   Yes, if depreciation exceeds gross investment (which, while improbable, is more likely to occur than the preceding condition).

4. (a) 1982   374.4; 17,390
       1985   489.8; 19,435
       1989   115.2; 26.2
   (b) 73.6; 16.4; 12.3; 2.7
       74; 33; 10.6; 4.7

5. The CPI is based on the items purchased, and their relative importance in the total purchases, for the majority of Canadian consumers. Since both university students and Saskatchewan are likely different from the national average, the CPI for Canada is only a rough measure of changes in the cost of living for the typical student at the U. of S.

CHAPTER 6

Multiple-Choice

1. b	2. d	3. c	4. c	5. b	6. b
7. d	8. b	9. c	10. b	11. c	12. b
13. d	14. c	15. b	16. b	17. b	18. c
19. d	20. c	21. d			

True/False

1. Uncertain; there is no logical necessity for purchasers of an economy's output to wish to buy exactly the amount produced. For example, consumers may choose to save some of their incomes.

2. True; lower corporate taxes would increase the expected yield on investment.

3. False; autonomous investment depends on factors other than the level of national income.

4. True; increased saving at any income reduces consumption, resulting in lower aggregate expenditure and national income.

5. True; firms adjust output to maintain inventories at the desired level.

6. False; any level of national income is potentially the equilibrium level, depending on desired aggregate expenditure.

7. False; it represents the equilibrium level of national income associated with each price level.

8. True; the higher the price level, the lower the planned aggregate expenditure.

9. True; the aggregate supply curve would shift in response to changes in input prices.

Problems

1. (a) greater than; decreases; remains constant; *JH/AB* or *KJ/BC* or *KH/AC*
   (b) *HG*; zero; *LK*
   (c) positive; *LK/BC/* or *GH/AB*
   (d) the new *C* curve is parallel to the original curve and intersects the 45° line at *M*.
   KJ/BC; *OL/OC*; remained constant; increased
   (e) the same as; *OC*

2. (a) *AE:*   56   65   73   80   86   91
   MPC: .9   .8   .7   .6   .5
   Multiplier: 10   5   3.3   2.5   2
   (b) $80; $4; 2.86 [*MPC* at 80 is .65]
   (c) 82.86; 65.86 [if multiplier estimated as 2.86]
   (d) $4 [with a multiplier of approx. 2.5 over range from $80 to $90 billion]

3. (a) 5
   (b) 60; 12
   (c) 12
   (d) No; increase in GDP would be only $12 billion
   (e) Yes; $12 billion and multiplier of 5 leads to $60 billion increase

4. (a) GDP decreases due to *AE* decrease
   (b) GDP increases; increase in *APC* at given GDP implies an upward shift in *AE* and incease in GDP
   (c) GDP increases; effect is to increase *AE* at given GDP.

5. (a) 150
   (b) 1.5
   (c) 35
   (d) The new *AE* curve would slope upward from the 100 intercept on the vertical axis, with a steeper slope than the original *AE*.
   (e) 167

CHAPTER 7

Multiple-Choice

1. c	2. c	3. b	4. b	5. a	6. a
7. c	8. c	9. c	10. b	11. b	12. c
13. b					

True/False

1. False; the M1 component (and all other categories of money supply) exclude federal government deposits.

2. False; the Bank of Canada can influence the Bank Rate only indirectly, through purchases of new treasury bills, since the Bank Rate is set at 0.25 per cent above the average yield rate on treasury bills.

3. Uncertain; any increase in the money supply will depend on the ability of chartered banks to lend out the increase in chartered bank reserves.

4. True; money includes the deposits created by banks when they lend, but does not include the reserves created by the Bank of Canada.

5. True; the deposit expansion factor is the reciprocal of the reserve ratio or fraction, but this factor expresses the maximum possible expansion.

6. False; the foreign banks are currently restricted by the Bank Act to holding a maximum of 16 per cent of the assets in the banking system.

Problems

1. (a) [example]
   (b) Chartered banks (A) loans + 100 (L) dep + 100
   Public (A) dep + 100 (L) loans + 100
   (c) Bank of Canada (A) sec + 1000 (L) res + 1000
   Chartered banks (A) sec − 1000, res + 1000 (ex.r. + 1000)
   (d) Chartered banks (A) res − 400, res + 400 (L) dep − 400, dep + 400, Public (A) dep − 400, dep + 400
   (e) Bank of Canada (L) dep − 500, res + 500
   Chartered banks (A) res + 500 (ex.r. + 450) (L) dep + 500

2. (a) [example]
   (b) final effect is indeterminate because this is simply a step in the expansion process
   (c) Bank of Canada (A) sec + 1000 (L) res + 1000
   Chartered banks (A) sec − 1000, res + 1000, loans + 10,000 (L) dep + 10,000
   Public (A) dep + 10,000 (L) loans + 10,000
   (d) no further change because initial changes simply cancel
   (e) Bank of Canada (L) dep − 500, res + 500
   Chartered banks (A) res + 500, loans + 4500 (L) dep + 5000
   Public (A) dep + 4500 (L) loans + 4500 [note: Govt. of Can. deposits not included in Public]

3. (a) Bank of Canada (A) sec − 100K (L) res − 100K
   Chartered banks (A) res − 100K (L) dep − 100K
   Public (A) sec + 100K, dep − 100K; reserve deficiency of $90K
   (b) $90 K; $90K reserves; $90K Bank of Canada advance (or loan); $90K advance to chartered banks; $90K reserves; fall; $10K; fall; $100K; decreased; $100K
   (c) $900K; $900K; fallen; $100K; fallen; $1 million; decreased; $1 million
   (d) loan reduction
   (e) $600 million
   (f) $5.45 billion; $5.45 billion; $5.45 billion (reserves of $6 billion will cover 6 × 100/$11 billion in deposits = $54.55 billion. Reduction in deposits is $60 − 54.55 billion = $5.45 billion).

CHAPTER 8

Multiple-Choice

1. b	2. c	3. d	4. c	5. c	6. b
7. a	8. c				

True/False

1. True; increased aggregate expenditure increases national income and thus the demand for money. As bonds are sold to increase money balances, bond prices fall and interest rates rise.

2. Uncertain; the increased supply could be more than offset by increased demand such that interest rates increase, causing velocity to increase.

3. True; this inverse relationship is logically true since the nominal or stated interest rate becomes a smaller fraction of the increased price.

4. Uncertain; increased national income will increase the demand for money, but the quantity actually held or "supplied" will depend on monetary policy. With no change in supply, the increased demand will increase the interest rate.

5. False; inelasticity implies proportionately less effect but not the absence of an effect, unless one assumes the extreme and improbable case of perfect inelasticity.

Problems

1. (a) 3
   (b) a 5 per cent increase in the price level (or $P = 105$)
   (c) M could increase by 10 per cent, or $2,000; a fall in the price level to $P = 90.9$

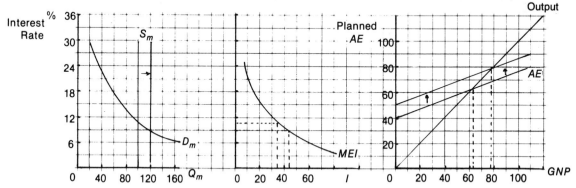

2. (a) 9
   (b) increase; 10; elastic; 1.25 [$(1\%) \times (9 + 11)/(35 + 45)$]
   (c) increase; 10; increase; 15; 1.5; $\frac{1}{3}$

CHAPTER 9

Multiple-Choice   1. a   2. d   3. d   4. c   5. c   6. b
7. c   8. d

True/False

1. False; the Phillips curve shows that a decrease in inflation can be associated with an increase in unemployment.

2. Uncertain; the future burden of the debt depends on whether the original funds were used to increase productive capacity that would generate the additional income to repay the debt.

3. True; the Bank of Canada would be creating new money to lend to the federal government, so consumers and businesses would continue to spend rather than be induced to lend to the government.

4. True; frictional unemployment tends to increase under better economic conditions because people are more willing to leave current jobs in order to look for better jobs and because more people enter the labour market to look for a job.

Problems   1. (a)

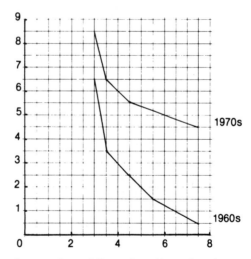

(b) 2.5; 5.5; 1.0
(c) move the economy along the curve; aggregate expenditure
(d) shift the curve inward; structural

2. (a) 75; .75; 4

(b) increase; 3.0; decrease; 4.0; 12.0

CHAPTER 10

Multiple-Choice
1. c	2. b	3. d	4. c	5. a	6. b
7. b	8. b	9. d			

True/False

1. False; one cannot draw any firm conclusions about policy simply by observing interest rate changes. Other factors may be offsetting policy actions.

2. True; this is likely to occur because an increase in the money supply usually leads to a lower rate of interest, and this causes a shift of short-term deposits from Canada to foreign financial institutions.

3. False; there are lags in the effect of monetary policy, just as there are with fiscal policy.

4. True; the greater the elasticity of investment with respect to interest rates, the greater the change in investment for a given change in the money supply, and, hence, in the interest rate.

5. True; when a contractionary money supply makes it more difficult to borrow, near-money (e.g. bonds) becomes available to meet these demands.

6. False; expansionary periods are usually associated with low interest rates; but velocity is usually greatest with high interest rates, because persons hold smaller account balances.

7. Uncertain; under a fixed exchange rate system, monetary policy may be used to change interest rates and thus influence the foreign exchange rate; but under a truly flexible exchange rate system, the monetary policy would be directed to domestic conditions only.

8. False; arbitrage refers to the simultaneous buying and selling in two different markets to take account of price differences.

9. Uncertain; the slope of such a supply curve depends on the elasticity of demand for the imports.

10. True; the Bank of Canada acts in this case as the agent for the Government of Canada.

11. False; under a fixed exchange rate system, monetary policy is required to deal with this external policy as well as the domestic conditions — including unemployment and slow growth, as well as inflation.

12. False; the government has intervened, through the Bank of Canada, to moderate abrupt changes in the foreign exchange rate.

13. True; the focus of monetary policy has alternated, but *not* in a uniform cycle.

Problems

1.

	Demand	Supply	Exchange Rate	Quantity
(a)	−	0	−	−
(b)	+	0 or −	+	+ or ?
(c)	+	0	+	+
(d)	−	0	−	−

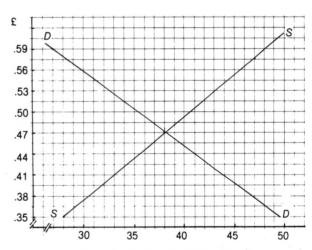

Canadian Dollars for British Pounds
(billions of dollars per month)

2. (a) C$1.00 = £0.47
   (b) approx. £0.45
   (c) approx. £0.49 (or .485)
   (d) approx. £0.49 (or .495)
   (e) The government would need to supply $10 billion per month to this foreign exchange market by offering to purchase British pounds.

CHAPTER 11

Multiple-Choice   1. a   2. c   3. a   4. c   5. d   6. c
7. a

True/False

1. False; monetary and fiscal policies are intended primarily to affect aggregate expenditure, but inflation and unemployment are caused by other factors in addition to demand.

2. Uncertain; it is generally true that rising interest rates curtail inflation by reducing consumption and investment spending. But higher interest rates also add to seller's or cost-push inflation.

3. True; an increase in the money supply is available for an increase in spending, as well as inducing more investment spending through lower interest rates.

4. False; the objective of a "rules" or "targets" policy is to increase the money supply at a prescribed rate, usually related to the expected rate of real economic growth.

5. False; monetarists and Keynesians also disagree on the normative issue related to the extent of government intervention in the economy.

6. True; labour supply policies are intended to reduce cost-push inflation resulting from wage increases where there are labour shortages, and to reduce unemployment by training workers for new jobs.

7. False; a prices and incomes policy is intended only to reduce inflation; it can have no direct effect on unemployment.

CHAPTER 12

Multiple-Choice   1. b   2. d   3. b   4. d   5. d   6. a
7. b   8. c   9. b   10. d   11. b

True/False

1. True; when the labour force increases faster than the increase in physical capital, labour productivity is likely to decline because labour has relatively less capital to use in producing goods and services.

2. False; economic growth was due to both more labour and improved labour productivity. Foreign investment was only a minor factor in the latter component.

3. True; the *level* of labour productivity has increased gradually, but the *rate* of increase has declined. In other words, labour productivity has continued to improve, but much more slowly.

4. True; higher oil prices led to adoption of technology that used less energy, but was also less efficient.

5. False; real GDP is generally higher than nominal GDP for the years before the base year (since prices in those years were usually lower than in the base year).

6. False; the value for total-factor productivity will always be less than for labour productivity, because the numerator (GDP) is the same in each case, but the denominator is larger for total-factor productivity (since it includes both labour and capital).

7. Uncertain; the effect of the one per cent *difference* depends on the growth rate: with a 1 per cent growth rate, the total output doubles in 72 years, compared with 36 years for a 2 per cent growth rate; but the difference in doubling time between an 8 per cent and 9 per cent growth rate is only one year.

8. True; during the past two decades, Canada has spent about 1.5 per cent of GDP on research and development, while other industrialized countries have spent about 2 to 2.5 per cent.

Problems

1. (a) $200 billion [$300 billion $\times \frac{100}{150}$]

 (b) $10,000 [$200 billion $\div$ $20 million]
 (c) 1.33 [$300 billion $\div$ $225 billion]

2. 12; 24; 72

3. 2% [$1.015 \times 0.995 \times 1.02 \div 1.01 = 1.02$]

CHAPTER 13

Multiple-Choice	1. b	2. c	3. a	4. c	5. b	6. d
	7. b	8. a	9. c	10. b	11. a	12. d
	13. c	14. a	15. a	16. c	17. a	18. d

True/False

1. True; devaluation will not reduce the deficit if other countries also devalue and/or there is an inelastic demand for imports and exports.

2. True; the balance of payments is balanced by the changes in official reserves of gold and foreign currencies.

3. True; the principle of comparative advantage applies to any level of the production process, including different employees within a single firm.

4. False; the tariff is beneficial to the importing country only to the extent that the government increases its tax revenue, but this effect is offset by the higher prices consumers pay to support a less efficient industry in their own country.

5. False; the only valid economic argument is that tariffs may protect a growing ("infant") industry until it has a comparative advantage in its product.

6. True; Canadian products would then be cheaper for foreigners, who would increase the demand for Canadian products and hence increase the demand for labour.

7. False; speculation is also a problem under fixed exchange rate systems, particularly when speculators believe that a country has not devalued far enough and will be under pressure to devalue again.

8. False; even in this situation a country can benefit by specialization and trade.

Problems

1. (a) ⅓ kg of apples; ¼ kg of apples; 3 kg of wheat; 4 kg of wheat
   (b) apples and wheat; apples; nothing; wheat
   (c) 1A:3W and 1A:4W; apples; wheat
   (d) Yes. No trade would occur (because opportunity costs are equal) unless there are potential economies of scale to justify continued specialization.

(e)

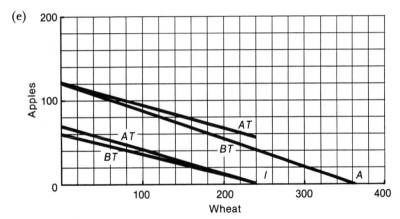

2. (a) 922; 1.00; 922

At the new exchange rate, the price of Canadian exports in US$ terms increases by $.10 (from .90 to 1.00) or by 11.1%. Since elasticity = 0.7, the quantity exported decreases by 7.8% (or 11.1 × .7). Therefore Canada sells 922 units for $922.

(b) 1,050, $.90, $945

The price of Canadian imports in C$ terms falls by $.10 (from 1.00 to .90) or by 10%. Since elasticity = 0.5, the quantity imported increases by 5% (or 10.0 × .5). Therefore Canada buys 1,050 units at $.90 for an expenditure of $945.

(c) balance [receipts and expenditures each = C$1,000]
deficit [$922 − $945 = $ − 23]

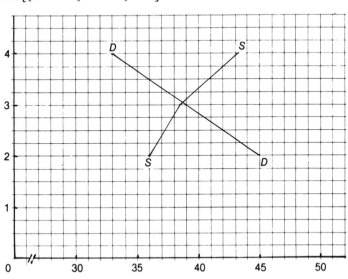

3. (a) price in C$: 72; 48; 36; C$ supplied: 36,000; 38,400; 43,200; Swiss francs demanded: 72,000; 115,200; 172,800

(b) price in SF: 6; 9; 12; C$ demanded: 45,000; 39,000; 33,000; Swiss francs supplied: 90,000; 117,000; 132,000

(c) elastic; inelastic

(d) approximately SF3.05/C$1

(e) excess demand for C$ and hence upward pressure on exchange rate; Canada would probably revalue and/or Switzerland would devalue.

   An export tax (with inelastic demand for whisky) would increase the quantity of Canadian dollars demanded, and thus would not be a solution. A tariff would reduce the quantity demanded both of Canadian whisky and of Canadian dollars (since the tariff is paid in francs to the Swiss government), and thus would relieve the excess demand for the Canadian dollar.

4. (a) capital   (d) invest. inc.   (g) goods
   (b) goods   (e) capital   (h) transfers
   (c) invest. inc. (f) services

5. (a) −1,000
   (b) −500
   (c)   0
   (d) −3,405,000

CHAPTER 14

Multiple-Choice   1. c   2. c   3. d   4. c   5. a   6. d
                       7. c   8. c   9. d   10. a

True/False   1. True; expenditures for these functions grew rapidly in the 1970s, and continue to account for the major part of government expenditures.

2. False; governments are also considered to have a role in resource allocation and economic stabilization.

3. True; benefit-cost analysis helps to show which programs realize the highest returns or benefits for a given expenditure.

4. Uncertain; "economic considerations" would include inter-provincial spillover effects that would suggest federal funding; but some programs might be provided more efficiently at local levels, where the needs or effects could be evaluated more precisely.

5. False; the "spillover benefits" argument is a case for financing by a higher level of government that spans the jurisdictions where spillovers occur.

6. Uncertain; whether it is easier to determine ability to pay, or benefits received, depends on the nature of the service in question.

7. Uncertain; "fairness" in a tax system is a normative matter and depends on the political views of the society.

8. True; sales taxes are considered indirect because they are borne by whoever purchases the commodity, rather than by specific groups of individuals.

9. False; the marginal tax rate increases as income increases.

Problems

1. (a)

Marginal Income	Marginal Tax Paid	Marginal Tax Rate (%)	Average Tax Rate	After-Tax Income
			0	0
2,000	200	10	10	1,800
3,000	450	15	13	4,350
3,000	750	25	17.5	6,600
4,000	1,200	30	21.67	9,400
8,000	2,800	35	27	14,600
20,000	8,000	40	33.5	26,600

(b) progressive
(c) $1,333
(d) four
(e) 35, 23.6

2. (a) *C*; *A*; *B*
(b) *A*
(c) more; less

CHAPTER 15

Multiple-Choice   1. b   2. d   3. d   4. a   5. d   6. b
7. c   8. a   9. c   10. d   11. d

True/False

1. False; an inferior good is one for which consumption decreases when income increases.

2. False; Engel's Law states that consumers spend a decreasing fraction of their incomes on food as income increases. This implies an elasticity greater than zero but less than one.

3. False; the concept of utility underlies the whole of consumer theory, and helps to explain the diminishing marginal rate of substitution.

4. True; consumer surplus is the difference between what consumers would be willing to pay and what they must pay to obtain the good.

5. True; indifference curves can never intersect because this would mean that a specific combination of goods provided two different levels of satisfaction—which is logically impossible.

6. True; since the marginal rate of substitution is the slope of the indifference curve, a diminishing rate of substitution results in a convex curve.

7. False; the budget line is a straight line because it represents the relative prices of the two groups of commodities in question, and these relative prices do not change as the individual changes the quantities purchased.

8. False; a higher level of satisfaction can be reached, with a given income, if there is a decrease in one or both prices.

9. True; the indifference curve slopes imply that Maria's marginal rate of substitution is such that giving up, say, three books can easily be compensated by gaining only one unit of clothing, so great is her marginal utility for clothing, while the opposite relationship is true for Ester.

Problems

1. (a) 4; 5
   (b) 6; 7; 4; 7
   (c) 90; yes; yes

2. (a) Figure 15.1

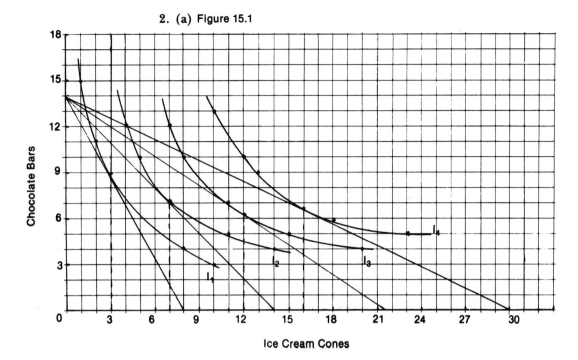

(b) 9; 3; [9 bars and 3 cones cost a total of $8.55]
(c) 3; 7; 12; 16
(d) 1.47; 1.24; 0.79 (note that elasticity decreases as the price declines)
(e) Figure 15.2

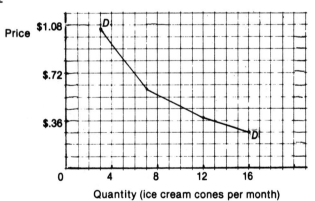

(f) 2; 2; 4

3. (a)   (b)

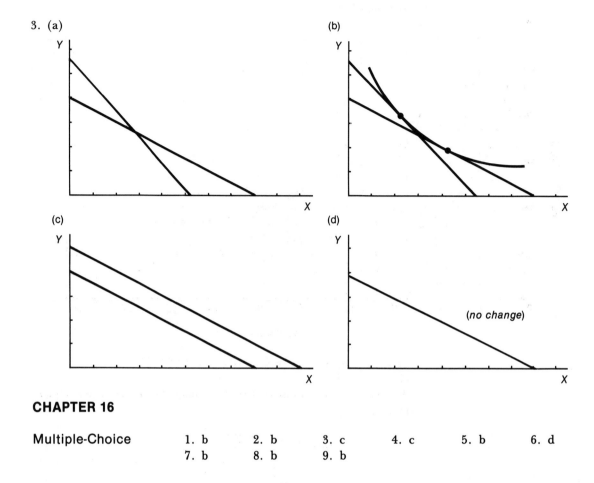

(c)   (d)

CHAPTER 16

Multiple-Choice   1. b   2. b   3. c   4. c   5. b   6. d
                        7. b   8. b   9. b

True/False   1. True; the short-run *ATC* decreases at low outputs due to the dominating effect of the declining *AFC*, but at larger outputs the *AFC* is dominated by the increasing *AVC* due to increasing *MC*.

2. False; the short-run *ATC* would be a straight line if there were no fixed costs and marginal cost was a constant. In this case *AVC* = *ATC*, and it is a straight horizontal line.

3. True; if marginal cost is less than average cost, this decreases average cost even if marginal cost is rising.

4. True; normal profit is part of total cost because it is part of the opportunity cost incurred to remain in the industry in question.

5. False; for this to occur, there would be no variable factors (which is extremely unlikely), or there would be no fixed factors, and therefore no long-run period.

6. True; the law of diminishing returns describes the result of combining one or more variable factors with a fixed factor.

7. True; average fixed cost must decline with increasing output because a fixed amount is being divided by an increasing number.

8. False; economies of scale refer to the lower average costs associated with increases in the fixed factor.

Problem   1.

(a)   (b)   (c)   (d)

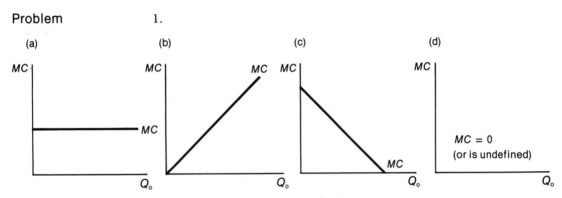

(e) The variable input is irrelevant to the production of the commodity in question; that is, no matter how much of the input is used, there is no change in the output. (But, of course, it is difficult to imagine a practical example of this.)

CHAPTER 17

Multiple-Choice   1. c   2. d   3. d   4. c   5. d   6. c

True/False   1. True; because the short-run supply curve is the marginal cost curve above the minimum AVC, and marginal cost usually increases due to the effect of decreasing productivity of variable factors.

2. False; when firms are not able to cover their fixed costs in the short run, they wish at least to minimize their losses.

3. True; the lower cost for building materials would increase housing supply and lower the price.

4. False; although minimum ATC is the most efficient level of output, it is usually not the most profitable level, namely where $MC = MR$.

5. False; a firm will produce in the short run even if realizing a loss, provided that the product price exceeds the AVC.

6. False; perfectly competitive firms operate in the long run at the minimum ATC, but excess capacity is defined as operating at a lower output and higher ATC.

7. True; the firm in a perfectly competitive market can sell any quantity at the prevailing market price. Consequently, the marginal revenue, which is the price, is also equal to the average revenue.

Problems

1. (a) *CEIH*; $0CHQ_3$; $0EIQ_3$
   (b) $0B$; $0Q_1$
   (c) $0Q_3$; *EFJI*; $0FJQ_3$
   (d) $0Q_2$; zero; all
   (e) no change in AFC; an upward shift in AVC, in ATC, and in MC; less than $0Q_2$; $0D$; a loss
   (f) possibly, if the cost increase caused the minimum AVC to exceed $0D$
   (g) an upward shift in AFC and ATC; no change in AVC and MC; $0Q_2$; $0D$; a loss; no, because price $0D$ exceeds AVC at $0Q_2$
   (h) output will be slightly less than $0Q_2$ (where the new $MR = MC$); and there will be a loss; no, because $0C$ is greater than AVC at this output.

2. (a) *AP*:   0; 4; 7.5; 11.67; 15; 16; 15.83; 15; 14.13; 13.22
      MP: 4; 11; 20; 25; 20; 15; 10; 8; 6

Table 17.2

L	Q	TFC	TVC	TC	MC	AFC	AVC	ATC
0	0	2000	0	2000		—	0	—
					125.00			
1	4	2000	500	2500		500.00	125.00	625.00
					45.45			
2	15	2000	1000	3000		133.35	66.65	200.00
					25.00			
3	35	2000	1500	3500		57.15	42.85	100.00
					20.00			
4	60	2000	2000	4000		33.30	33.30	66.60
					25.00			
5	80	2000	2500	4500		25.00	31.25	56.25
					33.35			
6	95	2000	3000	5000		21.05	31.60	52.65
					50.00			
7	105	2000	3500	5500		19.00	33.35	52.35
					62.50			
8	113	2000	4000	6000		17.70	35.35	53.05
					83.35			
9	119	2000	4500	6500		16.80	37.80	54.60

(b) Figure 17.2

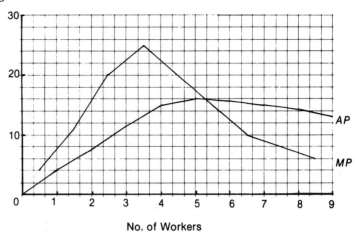

(c) Figure 17.3

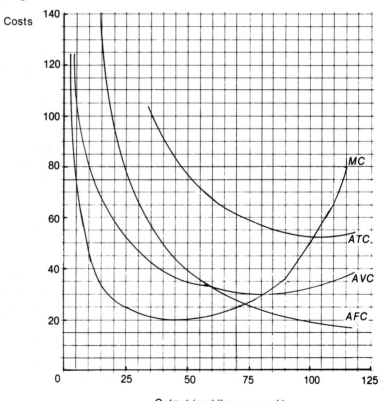

(d) 48; 3.5; 25

(e) 80; 5; 16

(f) 110; profit; 1,375; (12.50 × 110)

(g) $31.25; $52.35; 105

(h) 0; 93; 100; 108; 113; 115

(i) 0; 1860; 2000; 2160; 2260; 2300;

   $70; 2260; some pure profit; increase; decrease

3. (a) $110; 80; 68; 63; 65; 47; 39; 38; 41; 42; 44; 51; 51; 55; 67; 90

   (b) Figure 17.4

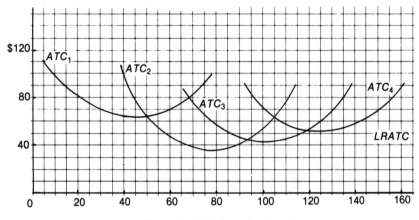

Quantity of Widgets Produced

4. (a) An increase in the wage rate increases the marginal cost and average total cost by an equal amount for each level of output, illustrated by the uniform vertical shift of the cost curves to MC_2 and ATC_2. As each firm reduces its output toward Q_2, where $MR_1 = MC_2$, the supply for the whole industry is decreasing, toward S_2. The short-run equilibrium will be at P_2 and Q_2 for the industry, and at P_2 and Q_3 for each firm, where it just covers its average variable cost. But at P_2, each firm is incurring a loss of $ATC_2 - P_2$, equal to its AFC.

   In the long run, enough firms will leave the industry (due to previous losses) that supply will decrease still further, until price rises to P_3, where firms are again just covering their total costs. The resulting equilibrium position for the firm is at the same output as before, Q_1, but at a higher price, P_3. Output in the industry declines to Q_3, due to the smaller number of firms.

(a) (i) in the short run:

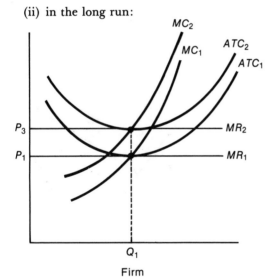

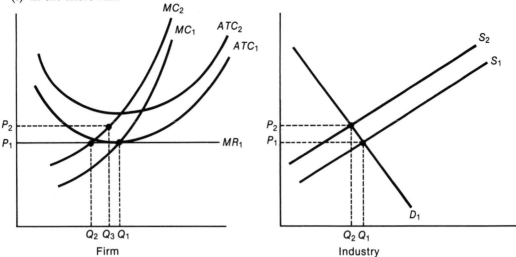

(ii) in the long run:

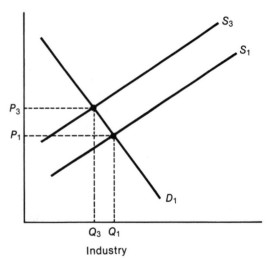

(b) An increase in demand for the commodity increases the price from P_1 to P_2, but there is also an increase in the quantity produced, from Q_1 to Q_2. At the higher price, P_2, each firm is realizing a profit $(P_2 - ATC_1)$ at Q_2. This profit attracts other firms into the industry, thus increasing the supply. This will continue until the price returns to P_1, where firms are again just breaking even. Each firm will produce Q_1, as before, but the increased number of firms results in a greater output by the industry, Q_3.

(b)   (i) in the short run:

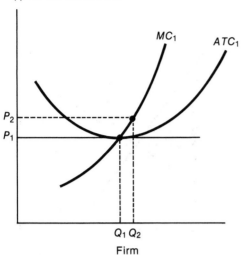

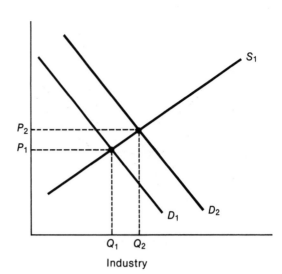

(ii) in the long run:

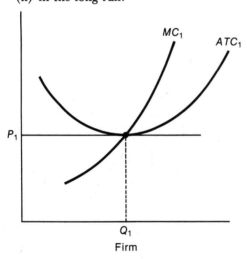

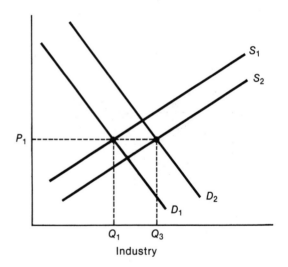

CHAPTER 18

Multiple-Choice   1. b   2. c   3. d   4. d   5. d   6. d

7. c   8. c   9. b   10. c   11. a   12. d

True/False   1. True; demand is inelastic when MR is negative.

2. False; a monopoly will realize a loss if ATC exceeds AR at the output where $MC = MR$.

3. True; a lump-sum subsidy is a fixed cost so does not affect *MC*, output, or price.

4. Uncertain; the profit may either increase or decrease with increased output.

5. True; undifferentiated-product oligopolies tend to act as monopolies, otherwise they must try to differentiate their products.

6. False; changes in fixed costs have no effect on price since the profit-maximizing output is affected only by variable costs.

7. False; although variable costs do affect profit-maximizing output and price, an increase in variable costs may result in a loss—which would be of great concern to a monopolist.

Problems

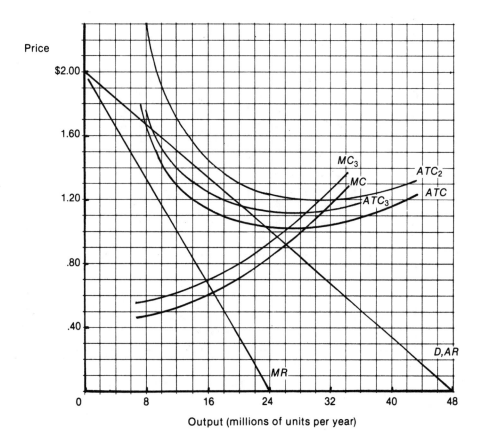

Output (millions of units per year)

1. (a) 17; $1.30; $22,100,000; 24
   (b) $1.12; $19,040,000; $.18 [1.30 − 1.12]; $3,060,000
   (c) 8; 22
   (d) non-existent; the monopolist sets the price—it does not respond to the market prices by deciding what quantity to produce at a given market price
   (e) no change in *MC* curve because the $5.1 million is a fixed cost, *ATC* curve shifts upward by the amount of the change in *AFC*; 17; loss; $2,040,000 (*ATC* increases by $.30 at 17 million units, hence there is a loss of $.12 per unit at 17 million units)
   (f) *MC* and *ATC* curves each shift up by $.10 at all quantities; 16; $1.32; profit $1,280,000 ($.08 per unit on 16 million units)
   (g) 26; $1.04; $27,040,000; $37,960,000 [(26 m. × $.92) + ½ (26 m. × $1.08)]; $10,920,000; $7,860,000

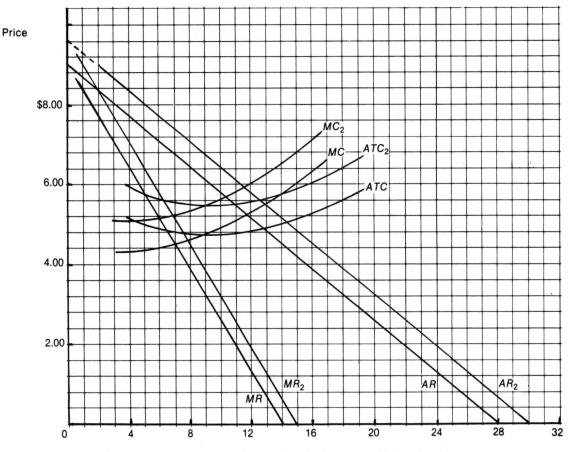

Pizzas (thousands per month)

2. (a) 7; $6.80; $4.80; $14,000
   (b) 7,000; $7.40; $5.60; $12,600
   (c) *MR*; *AR*; zero

CHAPTER 19

Multiple-Choice   1. d   2. a   3. c   4. b   5. d   6. b

True/False

1. False; there is no reason for demand to change as the firm adjusts from its short-run to its long-run equilibrium.

2. Uncertain; the firm may realize a profit or incur a loss in the short run.

3. True; a monopolistically competitive firm produces a lower output and at a higher average cost, than does the perfectly competitive firm, in equilibrium.

4. False; a firm that exists as a monopoly need fear no competitors because the conditions that created the monopoly will prevent others from entering that industry.

5. False; an oligopolistic firm faces only a few competitors, whereas a monopolistically competitive firm has several competitors.

6. False; the optimum rate of output is the level at which average cost is at a minimum.

7. False; perfectly competitive firms have no incentive to innovate because their competitors will immediately copy their innovation.

8. True; oligopolies can enhance their competitiveness by creating differentiated products, often at very little additional cost.

Problem   1.

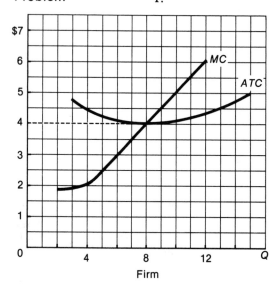

Firm

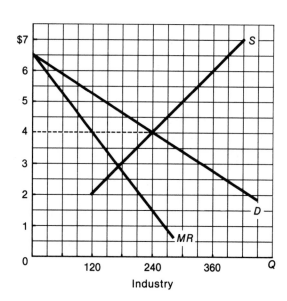

Industry

(a) The industry's supply curve is the sum of the identical supply curves for the 30 firms in the industry; $4; 240

(b) 170; $4.75

(c) higher; $0.75; 70; less

(d) The consumers' surplus is the area under the demand curve, above $4.00 in the case of perfect competition; and above $4.75 in the case of monopoly.

CHAPTER 20

Multiple-Choice   1. c   2. c   3. d   4. b   5. c   6. c
                       7. b   8. c

True/False   1. True; the concentration ratio measures the extent to which the largest firms in the industry dominate the industry, in terms of output, employees, or assets.

2. Uncertain; in large corporations that have a great number of shareholders, control may be possible with only 30 per cent of the shares; but where there are only a few shareholders, it may be necessary to hold 51 per cent.

3. False; the Competition Act is intended to prevent the formation of monopolies but does not deal with existing monopolies.

4. False; a natural monopoly occurs when a firm's optimum size is so large, relative to the total market, that only one or two firms can operate efficiently.

5. Uncertain; the statement correctly describes the intent of regulatory agencies but some agencies no longer have responsibility for setting prices or rates.

6. False; licensing restricts competition by reducing the number of potential suppliers of a service.

Problem

1. (a) 96.9%
   (b) oligopoly; two firms (A and B) dominate the industry, with 85 per cent of the sales.
   (c) Yes, B + D would have $8 million in sales, which is less than firm A and represents only ⅓ of the industry.
   (d) No, the existence of other firms of relatively small size suggests that economics of scale can be realized by several firms in the industry.

CHAPTER 21

Multiple-Choice

1. b	2. c	3. a	4. a	5. d	6. b
7. a	8. b	9. c	10. b	11. d	12. d
13. c					

True/False

1. Uncertain; the relative size of government payments under each scheme depends on the price elasticity of demand. Inelastic demand requires larger government payments under the deficiency payments scheme.

2. Uncertain; production restrictions increase incomes only if demand is inelastic.

3. False; the cobweb theorem explains price fluctuations due to lagged output responses to previous price levels.

4. True; the demand for farm products, as a group, is inelastic because they are necessities.

5. Uncertain; although the prices of some products that are subject to "hog cycles" may return to a long-run "normal" price, there is no logical reason to expect this to happen. Other changes in supply or demand will also influence the price.

6. False; provincial marketing boards are not responsible for price support programs; rather, these boards regulate the production and sale of the commodity in question.

7. False, the rotation decision depends on the rate of harvesting compared with the rate at which the forest can naturally replace itself.

8. False; about 20 per cent of the fish is consumed in Canada and about 80 per cent is exported.

9. Uncertain; in principle, the maximum sustainable yield should be a good guide to fish quotas, but there are several practical limitations to its use.

10. Uncertain; it depends on what is meant by "Canadian oil": the price of exported Canadian oil was allowed to rise to the world price, while oil for domestic consumption was priced at the pre-OPEC level.

11. True; there is not a "world price" for natural gas because there is not a worldwide market, due to the high cost of long-distance transportation of natural gas.

Problems

1. (a)   (b)

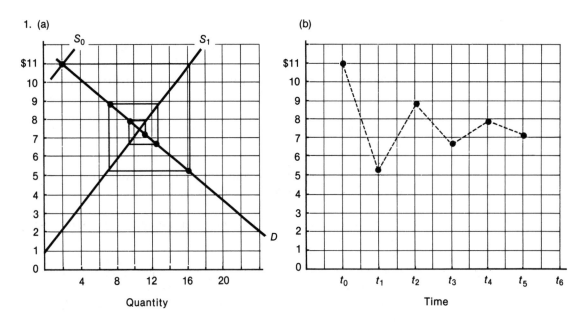

(c) The fluctuations occur because the producers make their decisions about the quantity of output in response to the current market price. When the price for potatoes was at $5.50 per 100 kg, producers decided to produce only 7,000 kg, but this amount could be sold for $8.50 per 100 kg. This higher price, in turn, led to an output of 12,000 kg. The fluctuations began, however, because the supply conditions changed, and moved the market away from equilibrium.

(d) If the demand were less elastic, the fluctuations would be greater; but if supply were less elastic, the fluctuations would also be less. Try to show this by imposing alternative demand and supply curves on the diagram for 1(a). (In a separate diagram, show that the market will return to equilibrium more quickly, the more elastic is demand and the less elastic is supply.)

(e) Yes, a change of either supply or demand will disturb the market and will provoke a fluctuation in the prices and quantities.

CHAPTER 22

Multiple-Choice   1. c   2. c   3. c   4. b   5. a   6. d

True/False

1. True; the prices received by productive factors for their services, when multiplied by the number of units of service, determine factor incomes. For example, a labourer's wage rate multiplied by the number of hours worked yields the total income for the period.

2. True; because each additional unit would increase the total profit.

3. False; the firm's demand for a factor's service is the same as the marginal revenue product.

4. False; the marginal resource cost increases as the quantity of inputs increases and, hence, as output increases.

5. False; the *MRP* is the additional revenue from each additional unit of input.

6. True; inelastic demand for the product tends to create inelastic demand for its labour input, since a higher product price only slightly reduces quantity sold.

Problems

1. (a) *TR* 0   120.00   201.60   249.60   268.80   264.00   240.00
         MR 120.00   81.60   48.00   19.20   -4.80   -24.00
   (b) 2; 3
   (c) imperfectly

2. less; more

3. (a) *MRP* schedules are the same as *MPP* schedules because firm sells product for $1.00 per unit at all output levels
   (b) 5; 7
   (c) 3; 5

CHAPTER 23

Multiple-Choice

1. b   2. c   3. d   4. b   5. d   6. d
7. b

True/False

1. True; real wages decrease if the inflation rate exceeds the percentage increase in nominal wages.

2. False; labour force participation rate measures the actual labour force as a percentage of the potential labour force.

3. False; an economy's long-run labour supply depends on its net immigration flows, as well as the birth rate and death rate.

4. False; the marginal revenue product could conceptually be a constant value, but this would occur under the very unusual case where marginal physical product is constant, with a straight-line total product curve. (See Answer to Chapter 16, Problem 1(a)).

5. True; this is the case in a "one-company town" or where virtually everyone in a specific occupation is employed by the government.

6. False; the marginal cost of hiring an additional worker is the wage to hire that person, plus the addition to the total wage bill required to bring all workers previously hired up to the new wage level.

7. True; both firms may be employing labour in the same labour market and may employ such a small share of the total labour supply that they have no effect on the wage rate.

8. True; the firm should increase the amount of labour employed until the marginal revenue product is just equal to the wage rate, i.e., the cost of an additional unit of labour in a perfectly competitive labour market.

9. Uncertain; the substitution effect dominates at low wage levels and the income effect dominates at high wage levels.

Problems

1. (a) *TRC*: 0 2 6 12 20 30 42 56 72 90
   MRC: 2 4 6 8   10 12 14 16 18
   (b)

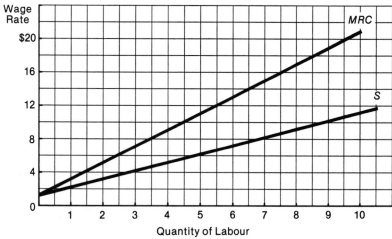

(c) ¼ ; ½ ; 2

2. (a) K; Q_2; W_2
   (b) L; M; Q_1; W_1; W_1; W_2; W_3

CHAPTER 24

Multiple-Choice

1. b   2. c   3. c   4. c   5. d   6. d
7. c   8. d

True/False

1. False, craft unions are based on a specific trade or occupation, while industrial unions are based on a specific industry or a group of related industries.

2. False; less than one-half of the unionized workers in Canada belong to an international union.

3. True; all unions aim to increase their wage rates, but unions differ with respect to other goals.

4. False; an employee can be represented by only one union or bargaining agent.

5. False; collective bargaining legislation generally provides for a conciliation stage, in which a conciliation officer is appointed by the labour relations board to try to reach an agreement.

6. True; unions differ widely, depending on time, region, and industry, in their impact on wages.

7. False; labour legislation is also the responsibility of the federal government, with respect to national or interprovincial industries such as banking and transportation, and for other specific aspects of labour relations.

Problems

1. (a) perfectly elastic supply (i.e., a horizontal line) at $5.60
   (b) 3
   (c) 2; less; 112; elastic
   (d) increase; more; rise; less than

2. (a) imperfect; the supply curve facing the firm is not perfectly elastic
   (b) 320; $6.60; $10.80; less than
   (c) bilateral monopoly; $11.60; $6.80; the relative bargaining strength of the union and the employer; a perfectly competitive labour market

CHAPTER 25

Multiple-Choice   1. b   2. b   3. b   4. b   5. a

True/False

1. True; a factor must receive an amount at least equal to what it would earn in an alternative use.

2. True; all of its payment would be transfer earnings.

3. False; the reverse is true. That is, the value of the land depends on the price paid for its use.

4. True; economic rent, as the difference between what users are willing to pay and what landowners require to make the land available, increases with the greater demand and higher price for land's use.

5. False; interest rates include a "return to waiting" (i.e., the rate of time preference) and expected inflation, as well as estimated risk.

6. False; the present value could remain constant or increase if the price of the product of the capital asset were to increase.

Problem

1. (a) $200,000
   (b)

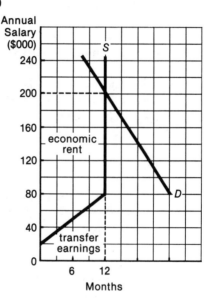

   (c) No effect on supply (or demand). The vertical supply curve indicates that the player would play for the full year for any amount over $80,000 per year.
   (d) The tax could be $120,000 per year, for the reason given above.

CHAPTER 26

Multiple-Choice   1. a   2. c   3. d   4. d   5. d   6. c
                        7. b   8. c   9. b   10. d   11. b

True/False

1. False; labour income is the largest share (about 75 per cent) of the economy's total income.

2. False; there has been very little change in the poverty rate during the past 25 years (but of course the dollar definition of the poverty line increases each year with inflation).

3. False; the largest number of persons in poverty are in Ontario and Quebec (but these provinces also have the largest total populations).

4. True; about half of the heads of families in poverty are in the labour force and most of these are employees (rather than self-employed).

5. Uncertain; some grant programs are designed to maintain the work incentive by reducing grants at less than 100 per cent of additional employment income.

Problem   1. (a)

Total Income	Percentage of Total Income	Cumulative	Percentage of Population	Cumulative
$ 6,000	0.6	0.6	6	6
54,000	5.4	6.0	18	24
100,000	10.0	16.0	20	44
264,000	26.4	42.4	33	77
96,000	9.6	52.0	8	85
180,000	18.0	70.0	9	94
300,000	30.0	100.0	6	100
1,000,000	100.0		100	

(b)

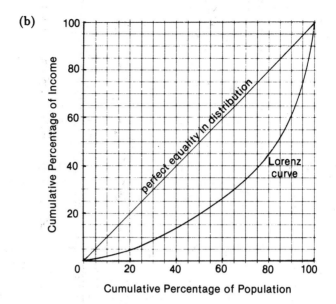

(c) no change in the income distribution or the Lorenz curve

(d)

After-Tax Income	Total Income Received	Percentage of Total Income	Cumulative
$ 1,000	6,000	0.8	0.8
2,700	48,600	6.6	7.4
4,250	85,000	11.4	18.8
6,400	211,200	28.4	47.2
9,000	72,000	9.7	56.9
14,000	126,000	17.9	74.8
32,500	195,000	26.2	100.0
	743,800		

Lorenz curve is shifted inward slightly.

(e) after-tax income is less unequally distributed, in the case of the progressive tax structure represented by (d), than in the proportionate structure represented by (c). This illustrates the importance of the tax structure in determining income distribution.

CHAPTER 27

Multiple-Choice   1. b   2. d   3. d   4. b

True/False

1. False; if the wage rates in the Atlantic provinces were at the national average, the industrial composition would result in above-average incomes.

2. False; the relative income differences have gradually narrowed. The per capita income in the poorest provinces was less than one-half of the income in the richest provinces in 1951. By 1988, this ratio had increased to about three-fifths.

3. Uncertain; there is no consistent relationship between the size of the capital/worker ratio and the capital/output ratio.

4. True; equalization payments are made by the federal government to the lower-income provinces to offset their lower tax bases.

5. False; fiscal policies, and especially monetary policies, have a nation-wide impact. In fact, they may have an adverse effect on the regional income differences.

6. True; the original protective tariff for manufacturing was more beneficial for Ontario and Quebec, where manufacturing was concentrated, than for the Atlantic provinces.